THIS BOOK
BELONGS TO

Previous page: Primatologist Dr. Jane
Goodall in Gombe Stream National Park,
Tanzania, in 1965

NATIONAL
GEOGRAPHIC
KiDS

THE BOOK OF
Heroines
TALES OF HISTORY'S GUTSIEST GALS

STEPHANIE WARREN DRIMMER

NATIONAL GEOGRAPHIC
WASHINGTON, D.C.

Contents

Introduction

HERE SHE COMES TO SAVE THE DAY

WHEN MANY HEAR THE WORD "HERO," THEY PROBABLY THINK OF A MUSCULAR MAN IN A CAPE, swooping down from the sky to rescue a damsel in distress. But real-life heroes don't have to wear costumes or have superpowers. And not all of them are men. Though heroines may not get as much screen time or space on the page as their manly counterparts, history is bursting with brave women who changed the world.

WHAT SEPARATES THE HEROINES FROM THE REST OF THE HERD? All tend to share these same seven stupendous qualities:

1. HEROINES STEP UP: When help is needed, true heroines are the first to raise their hands and volunteer for the job.

2. HEROINES ARE BRAVE: No one goes down in history by being cautious. A true heroine always does the right thing—no matter how scared she gets.

3. HEROINES ARE CONFIDENT: When the women in these pages heard "You're not good enough," they went ahead and did it anyway.

4. HEROINES ARE SELFLESS: They put others first. Period.

5. HEROINES DO THE RIGHT THING: A strong sense of justice guides them.

6. HEROINES FACE RISK: Heroines act no matter what, even if that means facing humiliation, violence—or even terrible danger.

7. HEROINES NEVER QUIT: When the going gets tough, heroines don't back down; they rise to the challenge.

THINK YOU MIGHT HAVE THE RIGHT STUFF?

In the following pages, you'll read about heroic women who fearlessly faced down assassins, invading armies, and tornadoes. Some of these heroines were born centuries ago, others are just beginning their brave deeds, and still others are the stuff of legend. And besides the seven qualities listed above, they all have one thing in common: They started out just like you.

Once upon a time, every one of the incredible women in this book was an ordinary girl. Then one day, they made a choice that changed them from ordinary to extraordinary. Whether it was a chance to fight an evil enemy or travel to a place no one had gone before, when these dauntless damsels heard the call for courage, they bravely stepped forward and answered.

And the most incredible thing about the world's heroines? This book holds only a small fraction. *The Book of Heroines* is dedicated to all of them: the famous females, the lesser-known ladies—and most of all, the heroines of the future, waiting in the wings for their chance for greatness. When your turn comes, will you become one of them?

AS YOU READ THE BOOK OF HEROINES, WATCH FOR THESE FEARLESS FEATURES ...

DARING DUDE

Sure, this is a book about women, but that doesn't mean courageous chaps should be swept under the rug. These sidebars highlight some of history's greatest heroes.

Heroism isn't always planned. Jump into the extraordinary situations that drove people to make daring decisions in a hurry.

MOMENT OF BRAVERY

CHAPTER ONE

Leading LADIES

For centuries, most ambitious women were relegated to roles behind the scenes. But the heroic lady leaders in this chapter weren't satisfied to stay in the shadows of male kings and presidents. From ancient queens who ruled empires alone to modern trailblazers who redefined the roles of women in law and leadership, these courageous gals saw a chance to make a difference and stepped up to the challenge. And when women lead people, cities, and nations ... well, they just plain rule.

Liberian president Ellen Johnson Sirleaf waves to supporters in 2011.

Eleanor ROOSEVELT

POLITICAL PIONEER

Before Eleanor Roosevelt, most first ladies performed duties more domestic and social than political. But Eleanor, the wife of U.S. president Franklin D. Roosevelt, wanted to do even more with her position. She changed the role of the first lady forever—and for the better.

UP TO THE CHALLENGE

In 1921, Franklin, a state senator at the time, was diagnosed with polio—a disease that left him permanently paralyzed below the waist. Eleanor became more than Franklin's caretaker; she became his eyes and ears—and legs. In the early 1930s, she traveled tens of thousands of miles a year to meet with politicians; inspect the conditions of hospitals, mines, and slums; and make appearances on his behalf. Franklin came to rely on her sharp observations about what she learned on the campaign trail and, with her help, won the presidency in 1932.

When Eleanor Roosevelt arrived at the White House, she became a first lady of many firsts. She held the first ever press conferences given by a

> "GREAT MINDS DISCUSS IDEAS; AVERAGE MINDS DISCUSS EVENTS; SMALL MINDS DISCUSS PEOPLE."
> —ELEANOR ROOSEVELT

FEARLESS FACTS

➲ **BORN:** October 11, 1884, New York, New York, U.S.A. ➲ **DIED:** November 7, 1962, New York, New York, U.S.A. ➲ **OCCUPATION:** First lady, author, activist ➲ **BOLDEST MOMENT:** Giving a whole new meaning to the first lady's job

president's wife—more than 300 of them. She authored books and wrote a column called My Day about her opinions on social and political issues. It was syndicated to newspapers across the country, reaching more than four million readers at its height. And at a time when few married women had careers, Eleanor surprised many when she matched the president's yearly salary, earning $75,000 from lecturing and writing. She donated most of her earnings to charity.

Eleanor Roosevelt speaks to the American people in a radio broadcast during World War II (above left); with her husband, president-elect Franklin D. Roosevelt, in February 1933 (above)

SPEAKING OUT

Eleanor Roosevelt used her position to give a voice to people who didn't have one: women, children, African Americans, and the poor. She banned male reporters from attending her press conferences, forcing newspapers that wanted to cover her to employ female journalists. In March 1941, she challenged the stereotype that African Americans couldn't be good pilots by climbing into a plane with a black airman from Moton Field, the air base in Tuskegee, Alabama, U.S.A., and going for a ride.

Franklin D. Roosevelt's death, in 1945, didn't put a stop to Eleanor's political career. She was appointed by President Harry S. Truman as a delegate to the United Nations (UN), an organization of representatives from nearly every nation in the world that aims to maintain world peace and resolve international disputes. She helped write the Universal Declaration of Human Rights, a famous document that states that all human beings have basic rights, such as the right to life, liberty, free speech, and privacy. When the UN adopted the declaration, on December 10, 1948, Eleanor Roosevelt received a standing ovation.

MENDING A BROKEN NATION: DARING DUDE
Abraham Lincoln (1809–1865)

Abraham Lincoln was elected the 16th president of the United States in November 1860. But when he took office five months later, the states were no longer united. Conflict had been building for years between the northern and southern states over the issue of slavery, which Lincoln opposed. His election brought the issue to a boiling point. Eleven southern states seceded, or separated, from the Union and formed a new nation: the Confederate States of America. Lincoln was now president of a nation divided. He threw himself into making it whole again, leading the country through one of its worst periods—the Civil War, which cost more than 600,000 lives. Lincoln not only preserved the Union—he also abolished slavery and helped shape the modern economy.

WOMEN IN THE WHITE HOUSE
PHENOMENAL FIRST LADIES

Presidents get all the credit. But did you know that many of their right-hand women were inspiring leaders in their own right? Meet fabulous first ladies who acted as their president's most trusted advisers, brought overlooked causes to national attention, and proved that White House wives can be a powerful force for change.

UNOFFICIAL ADVISER: Abigail Adams (1744–1818)

In 1797, Abigail Adams was the first first lady to have held a government position: Twenty years earlier, while the United States was fighting for its independence from Great Britain, the Massachusetts Colony General Court had appointed her to question other Massachusetts women to find out who were patriots and who were still loyal to the British crown. (In her spare time, she had melted down pewter tableware to make bullets for Revolutionary War soldiers.) But Adams's most important role was as an unofficial adviser to her husband, President John Adams. She wrote him hundreds of letters offering her opinions on political and social issues—among them, arguing that women should be equal to men in the eyes of the law. He wasn't persuaded, but those letters are some of the earliest documents on women's rights.

LIFE OF THE PARTY: Dolley Madison
(1768–1849)

This first lady was born a Quaker, a strict religious group that believed women should be quiet and reserved, stay home, and wear muted colors such as gray and brown. But Madison was not your average Quaker. This clever first lady became famous for her social functions, engineering them as an opportunity to help her husband, President James Madison, meet powerful people. She was the life of the party, wearing flashy clothes like bright yellow dresses and head turbans. She also adorned the White House with American-made pieces that still give the home of the president its famous look today. Dolley Madison is also known for one of the most quick-thinking and courageous first lady acts of all time. (Find out what she did on page 26.)

MODERN ROLE MODEL: Michelle Obama
(1964–)

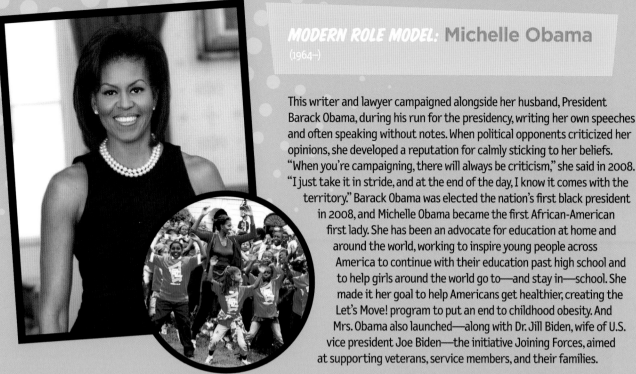

This writer and lawyer campaigned alongside her husband, President Barack Obama, during his run for the presidency, writing her own speeches and often speaking without notes. When political opponents criticized her opinions, she developed a reputation for calmly sticking to her beliefs. "When you're campaigning, there will always be criticism," she said in 2008. "I just take it in stride, and at the end of the day, I know it comes with the territory." Barack Obama was elected the nation's first black president in 2008, and Michelle Obama became the first African-American first lady. She has been an advocate for education at home and around the world, working to inspire young people across America to continue with their education past high school and to help girls around the world go to—and stay in—school. She made it her goal to help Americans get healthier, creating the Let's Move! program to put an end to childhood obesity. And Mrs. Obama also launched—along with Dr. Jill Biden, wife of U.S. vice president Joe Biden—the initiative Joining Forces, aimed at supporting veterans, service members, and their families.

CONSERVATION CHAMPION: "Lady Bird" Johnson (1912–2007)

This nature-loving first lady, wife of President Lyndon Baines Johnson, planted flowers and trees along roadsides to make cities and highways more beautiful. She championed conservation, encouraging America to protect its plants and wildlife. She was also an outspoken supporter of the civil rights movement, famously boarding a train called the Lady Bird Special in 1964 to tour eight southern states locked in racial turmoil and to make speeches supporting African-American rights. She spoke out for equal rights for women, too, calling it "the right thing to do." In 1977, she was given the Presidential Medal of Freedom, the highest award a United States citizen can earn.

FATHER OF THE COUNTRY: George Washington (1732–1799)

DARING DUDE

No, George Washington wasn't a first lady, but he was another kind of famous first: the nation's first president. Before that, he was a general in the American Revolutionary War. On Christmas night, 1776, General Washington led his force of roughly 2,400 Continental Army soldiers across the freezing Delaware River, dodging floating chunks of ice and paddling through bone-chilling sleet. His troops were dressed in rags and weary from defeat, but General Washington was desperate for a victory in the war for independence from England and thought a surprise attack via this dangerous route might catch the enemy off guard. He was right. Washington's victory was just one of many examples of Washington's trademark daring and leadership skills. When the war ended, he was the Founding Fathers' unanimous choice for the country's first president.

Elizabeth I

MARRIED TO HER COUNTRY

"BETTER BEGGAR WOMAN AND SINGLE THAN QUEEN AND MARRIED."
—ELIZABETH I

When Elizabeth I took the throne as the Queen of England in 1558, she had a tough job ahead of her. England's royals were regularly overthrown, imprisoned, and beheaded. Her country was fighting with France, and the war was quickly eating up the royal gold. On top of that, England was embroiled in an internal battle as its two religious groups, the Roman Catholics and the Protestants, clashed. The ruler before Elizabeth, her sister "Bloody" Mary, had only made matters worse by ordering hundreds of Protestants to be burned at the stake.

Undaunted, the 25-year-old royal clapped the crown on her head and met England's problems face-to-face. She ended the war with France, initiating an era of peace that lasted most of her reign. She also supported creative minds like author William Shakespeare, and the arts flourished under her rule. Unlike her sister, Elizabeth also supported religious freedom.

Many of Elizabeth's advisers wanted the queen to get married and have a child to take over the throne. But she didn't want to share her power with a husband—or lose it to him completely. From 1558 until her death in 1603, Elizabeth ruled alone in a world that was dominated by men. Through it all, Elizabeth was confident in her ability to lead as well as any male ruler could have, and she wasn't afraid to say so. "I know I have the body of a weak and feeble woman," she said, "But I have the heart and stomach of a king, and a king of England too!"

Under Elizabeth's rule, England became a major European power in politics, commerce, and the arts. Her 45-year reign was a time of peace and prosperity named the Elizabethan Age after the woman who made it happen.

FEARLESS FACTS

➲ **BORN:** September 7, 1533, Greenwich, England ➲ **DIED:** March 24, 1603, Richmond, England

➲ **OCCUPATION:** Queen ➲ **BOLDEST MOMENT:** Taking the throne in a tumultuous time

The Trung SISTERS

THEY FOUGHT FOR FREEDOM

Trung Trac and Trung Nhi were born two millennia ago in a small village in northern Vietnam. According to legend, their mother taught them—but not in the art of cooking and keeping house. She trained her daughters in the art of war.

For 150 years, Vietnam had been suffering under the rule of the much larger and more powerful country of China. In the year A.D. 36, the Han dynasty controlled Vietnam. To Dinh governed the region where the Trungs lived. He demanded bribes, raised taxes on necessities like salt, and even taxed Vietnamese peasants for fishing in the rivers.

The Trung sisters—now grown up—decided they had had enough of living under To Dinh's oppressive rule. So Trung Trac and her husband secretly plotted with local leaders to organize a revolt. But To Dinh got word of what they were plotting and had Trung Trac's husband killed.

Instead of giving up, Trung Trac and her sister came out swinging. They waged an attack against the Chinese that was fierce enough to kick them out of Vietnam. To Dinh himself was so scared of the dueling duo that he shaved off his hair to disguise himself and ran away! The Trung sisters ruled for two years, fiercely defending their country against the Chinese—but eventually they lost the battle. The Vietnamese still honor the bravery and sacrifice of the Trung sisters every year on the anniversary of their deaths.

THE VIETNAMESE STILL HONOR THE BRAVERY AND SACRIFICE OF THE TRUNG SISTERS.

FEARLESS FACTS

➔ **BORN:** ca A.D. 12, Jiaozhi, Vietnam ➔ **DIED:** ca 43, Vietnam ➔ **OCCUPATION:** Revolutionaries, rulers ➔ **BOLDEST MOMENT:** Fighting for Vietnam's independence from China

WOMEN OF THE WORLD
LEADING NATIONS AND MAKING HISTORY

These four savvy leaders took charge at pivotal moments in their countries' histories. They faced civil wars, economic crises—even assassination attempts! All dealt with doubters who said a woman couldn't be strong enough to head a nation. But each one went on to prove herself as a leader worthy of respect.

THE IRON LADY:
Margaret Thatcher (1925–2013)

When Margaret Thatcher was starting her political career, she once said, "I don't think there will be a woman prime minister in my lifetime." Little did she know at the time that the first female prime minister—the head of the United Kingdom's government—would be Thatcher herself.

When Thatcher stepped in as prime minister in 1979, many British citizens wondered if a woman would be strong enough to do the job. During her tenure, Thatcher faced a range of challenges: England's economy suffered, Argentina invaded British territory, and someone even tried to assassinate her. But she fielded each problem and was reelected twice, holding the position for more than 11 years. She was the first woman in modern times to lead a major Western power and the longest-serving British prime minister of the 20th century. Even those who disagreed with her respected her as Britain's Iron Lady, a powerful leader and a pioneering political force.

THE PEACEMAKER:
Ellen Johnson Sirleaf (1938–)

In the years leading up to her election as Liberia's first female president, Ellen Johnson Sirleaf had been imprisoned and forced into exile for criticizing her country's dictators. No one had thought she could win. But when she ran in 2005, the women of Liberia came out to support Sirleaf by the thousands because they believed she could bring peace to their country. Liberia had been torn apart by 14 years of civil war as opposing groups vied to control the government.

THE SCIENTIST TURNED POLITICIAN:
Angela Merkel (1954–)

Angela Merkel was trained as a physicist but became involved in politics in the late 1980s, when the Berlin Wall came down. In 2005, she became Germany's first female chancellor. She was a primary force in building the European Union, a group of 28 European countries that works together to maintain peace and grow the economy. In 2014, the German people elected her to a third four-year term, making her the longest-serving elected European head of state.

During her time in office, Merkel has kept Germany's economy strong while the world was mired in financial crisis, tackled energy reform, and used her influence to try and help the warring countries of Russia and Ukraine come to a peace agreement. She's developed a reputation as a strong, steady leader who carefully considers each decision. *Forbes* magazine has named her the most powerful woman in the world for ten years running.

THE NATION-MAKER: Golda Meir
(1898–1978)

Golda Meir was born to a Jewish family in the Ukrainian city of Kiev in 1898. It was a time and place in which there was extreme hatred against people of the Jewish faith. They were not allowed to own land, were forced to live in certain parts of the country, and were even attacked in riots. In 1903, deciding his family had endured enough, Golda's father moved them to America to live in Milwaukee, Wisconsin.

In 1933, when Adolf Hitler came to power, and through World War II, Jewish people living in Germany and other parts of Europe had to flee or risk death. But at the time, Jewish people had no official homeland to flee to. Meir had moved to Palestine in 1923 and was a politician working for Jewish rights. She helped found the state of Israel in November 1946 to give the Jewish people a land of their own. Over the span of just two years, between 1949 and 1950, 685,000 people came to live in the new state. Meir helped them find new jobs and places to live. Eventually, she became Israel's first female prime minister.

When she took office, the war-torn country was in shambles: The conflict had destroyed hospitals and caused teachers to flee, leaving a generation of children without education. There was no food or electricity, and the streets of the capital were lined with trash. But Sirleaf rose to the challenge, introducing free schooling, helping her country climb out of debt, and empowering Liberian women, earning her the Nobel Peace Prize in 2011. In a country struggling to rebuild, Sirleaf—the first female head of state of any nation in Africa and the world's first elected black female president—is a symbol of hope.

A Time(line)
FOR CHANGE

THE PATH TO AMERICA'S
FIRST FEMALE LEADERS

For well over a century, women have been making strides toward the highest office in the land. They've endured arrests, losses, criticism, and more, but they would not be thrown off course. Here are some history-making moments on their road to the White House.

1872
SUSAN B. ANTHONY is the first woman to vote (illegally) in a presidential election. She is arrested for breaking the law but refuses to pay the fine for her crime.

1916
JEANETTE RANKIN of Montana is the first woman elected to the U.S. House of Representatives.

1920
The **19TH AMENDMENT** of the U.S. Constitution gives women the right to vote.

1933
FRANCES PERKINS is appointed secretary of labor, making her the first woman to be in line for the presidency. (She's number 11 on the list.)

Senator **MARGARET CHASE SMITH** enters the race for the Republican presidential nomination. She shares a recipe for blueberry muffins at a press event, earning criticism for not taking the position seriously enough.

Democratic congresswoman **SHIRLEY CHISHOLM** becomes the first black woman to seek the presidential nomination from a major party. She doesn't win, but she views her attempt as a stepping-stone for those who would come after.

Congresswoman **GERALDINE FERRARO** becomes the first woman to be nominated for vice president. She and her Democratic Party running mate, Walter Mondale, lose the election. But a woman is closer than ever to becoming president.

HILLARY CLINTON, who had served as secretary of state during Barack Obama's presidency, again seeks the Democratic presidential nomination. As of the publication date of this book, she had won primary elections in multiple states—making her a strong contender for the top of the ticket.

Senator and former first lady **HILLARY CLINTON** loses the Democratic presidential nomination to Barack Obama, but it isn't a complete defeat: She's the first woman to win primary elections—the first being in New Hampshire. The same year, Sarah Palin runs for vice president on the Republican ticket.

Democratic congresswoman **PAT SCHROEDER** begins a campaign for the presidency but has to withdraw when she can't raise enough money.

Cleopatra

A GIRL RULER WITH GUTS

In ancient Egypt, it wasn't easy being pharaoh. Nations clashed with their neighbors in brutal wars. Floods and famine could wipe out entire civilizations. Pharaohs were often knifed by enemies or secretly poisoned by family members who wanted to rule. And pharaohs were almost always male. It would take a strong, smart, and ambitious woman to rule alone as a female pharaoh. Cleopatra was all of those things.

BECOMING QUEEN

The teenage Cleopatra got off to a rocky start. Her brother and co-ruler, Pharaoh Ptolemy XIII, had thrown her out of the palace and taken the crown for himself. Cleopatra was banned from her home—and her throne.

In the year 48 B.C., the general Julius Caesar was engaged in a civil war with another Roman leader, Pompey. Defeated in battle, Pompey fled to Egypt with Caesar hot on his trail. By the time Caesar arrived, Pompey had been assassinated—so the general set up camp in the Egyptian palace at Alexandria.

Cleopatra saw her chance to regain the throne. She knew that if she could get on Caesar's good side, the powerful Roman could help her get back in power. But she also knew there was no way Ptolemy's guards would let her into the palace. She had to meet with Caesar to win him over. But how? Cleopatra hatched a scheme. She had a servant wrap her up inside a carpet and then had the

> "I WILL NOT BE TRIUMPHED OVER."
> —CLEOPATRA

FEARLESS FACTS

⮑ **BORN:** ca 69 B.C. Alexandria, Egypt ⮑ **DIED:** August 12, 30 B.C., Alexandria, Egypt ⮑ **OCCUPATION:** Pharaoh ⮑ **BOLDEST MOMENT:** Rolling out of a carpet and onto the throne

carpet sent to Caesar as a gift, with her smuggled inside. When Caesar unrolled the carpet, out popped Cleopatra. Caesar was impressed by the young royal's courage and intelligence. By the time Ptolemy showed up, Cleopatra had charmed Caesar. With his help, she became the pharaoh of Egypt at age 17.

KEEPING THE CROWN

Together Caesar and Cleopatra grew very powerful. Caesar was even named Rome's dictator for life. But other Romans grew jealous of his position, and on March 15, 44 B.C., they assassinated Caesar. Without Caesar and his armies to support her, Cleopatra worried that someone might steal her throne.

In Rome, Caesar's assassins battled for power against Caesar's old friends. Both sides asked Cleopatra for her support. Cleopatra had to make a choice, and if she chose the wrong side, she could lose her position. She backed Caesar's supporters, and her bet paid off: They defeated their enemies and came to power.

One of these new rulers, Mark Antony, wanted to meet Cleopatra. The female pharaoh knew this was the time to impress the new Roman leader, so she sailed to the meeting in a luxurious ship, dressed to look like the goddess Isis. Her plan worked: Mark Antony fell instantly in love with her. Once again, she was united with one of the world's most powerful rulers. And, with his power to back her, she continued her reign as pharaoh.

Cleopatra ruled Egypt for almost three decades. Under her leadership, Egypt grew powerful and wealthy. In a time when even the world's mightiest men couldn't keep their thrones, Cleopatra used her brains and guts to become one of Egypt's greatest pharaohs.

Caesar meets Cleopatra in this 18th-century painting (above left); a bust depicting Cleopatra (above right)

ERASED FROM HISTORY: Hatshepsut (ca 1508–1458 B.C.)

Female pharaohs may have been rare, but Cleopatra wasn't the only one. Fourteen centuries before her, another queen ruled Egypt: Her name was Hatshepsut.

When Hatshepsut's husband died, the throne went to their infant son. Because he was too young to lead, Hatshepsut stepped in until he grew up. But seven years in, her ambition took over, and she declared herself pharaoh. To make herself appear more kingly, she had sculptures and engravings portray her as a man, with a beard and bulging muscles. After her death, her son finally came to power. Angry at his mother for keeping the throne for herself for so long, he had her image scraped from engravings and her statues smashed. As a result, it wasn't until the 19th century that scholars discovered evidence of this remarkable ruler.

GOING SOLO
THEY LOST THEIR KINGS BUT NOT THEIR COOL

Putting women in charge may seem like a new idea. As of 2015, there were fewer than 20 female leaders worldwide, with the majority of countries still yet to put a woman at the helm. But that doesn't mean women have always been passed over for positions of power. These brave gals were leading long, long ago.

ENTERPRISING EMPRESS: Zenobia (ca A.D. 240)

Syrian king Odaenathus didn't resist the Romans who controlled his lands. But when his wife Zenobia took the throne after he was assassinated around 267, she decided it was time to take the kingdom back. In 269, Queen Zenobia headed a revolt against the Romans; historians think she was only in her 20s at the time. She led her army to seize Egypt, then set off to conquer other lands. At the height of her power, she controlled important trade routes and issued coins stamped with her image. Before Emperor Aurelian defeated her around 274, she ruled an empire that stretched through present-day Syria, Lebanon, and Palestine.

REBEL RULER: Boudicca (ca A.D. 60)

When Boudicca's husband, the king of a Celtic tribe called the Iceni, died, Romans seized Boudicca's property. They cruelly beat her and her daughters. Boudicca and her people were angry, but they would not be broken. The furious queen gathered an army and plotted a rebellion. Some of her soldiers didn't even have weapons—they carried shovels and pitchforks into battle. But their ferocious female leader led them to kill 80,000 Romans. Though she was ultimately defeated, Boudicca is still celebrated today as a symbol of freedom and justice.

WARRIOR QUEEN: Artemisia (ca 500 B.C.)

Artemisia took power when her husband died, leading the people of Halicarnassus—then part of the Persian Empire—into war against the Greeks and proved herself as a cunning military leader. In 480 B.C., Artemisia personally commanded five ships in the Persian War's Battle of Salamis. Though her side lost the battle, the clever queen saved her ship by taking down her flags and ramming a passing Persian vessel. Fooled into thinking she was on their side, the Greeks let Artemisia and her crew escape to fight again. When her enemies found out their mistake, they were enraged that a woman would dare deceive them. They put out an award for her capture, making Artemisia the Greeks' most wanted woman. She's the only female ancient historian Herodotus credited with the virtue of courage, or *andreia*—literally translated as "manly spirit."

NO KING, NO PROBLEM:
Sammu-ramat (ca 800 B.C.)

Centuries before Cleopatra raised a few eyebrows by claiming the crown, Assyrian queen Sammu-ramat shocked everyone when she took the throne after the death of her husband. Legend mixes with fact in tales about her. Some stories even say she was raised by doves in the desert and once did battle with the sun (in the form of a god)! But here's one that's likely true: Sammu-ramat ruled for many years, conquered distant lands, and built Babylon, a famous ancient city whose ruins now lie in modern-day Iraq.

KING OF THE KNOWN WORLD: DARING DUDE
Alexander the Great (356 B.C.–323 B.C.)

Alexander became king at the age of 20. He died just 13 years later from a disease called malaria. But in those few years, he accomplished more than most leaders achieve during their entire lives. Alexander was a military commander who believed in leading by example, boldly charging into battle at the head of his armies. He never lost a fight, despite overwhelming odds. In just eight years, Alexander conquered the Persian Empire, Egypt (which he ruled as pharaoh), parts of what would become Iran and Iraq, and India. Along the way, he spread Greek culture, language, art, and architecture, while taking on the customs of his diverse subjects. For a brief time, Alexander ruled the world's largest empire. Today, more than 20 cities bear his name.

23

Condoleezza RICE

SHE ROSE ABOVE

Condoleezza Rice grew up in Birmingham, Alabama, U.S.A., in the 1960s, a time when the southern U.S. was plagued by racial turmoil. Blacks and whites were segregated, or kept separate, when using public restrooms, attending school, going to the movies—even when drinking from water fountains. Hatred and violence were never far away. When Condoleezza was eight years old, her friend and three other young girls were killed when members of an extremist group called the Ku Klux Klan bombed the 16th Street Baptist Church.

But Condoleezza didn't let fear hold her back. She studied hard, graduating from high school at age 16. Though she had dreamed of becoming a concert pianist, a college class sparked her interest in international politics, and she changed career paths, eventually earning a doctorate in political science.

Rice became an expert on the Soviet Union and, in 1989, was asked to share her knowledge by serving on the United States National Security Council. There, she impressed President George H. W. Bush with her intelligence and wisdom, and he began to rely on her advice. In 2001, President George W. Bush appointed her national security adviser. She was the first black woman—and second woman ever—to hold the post. She went on to become the first female African-American secretary of state in 2004. She was also the first African American and the first woman—and the youngest person—to lead Stanford University when she served as its provost from 1993 to 1999.

> "I'M QUITE CONVINCED THAT A LOT OF MY SUCCESS HAS BEEN BECAUSE I WAS DOING SOMETHING THAT I LOVED TO DO."
> —CONDOLEEZZA RICE

FEARLESS FACTS

➔ **BORN:** November 14, 1954, Birmingham, Alabama, U.S.A. ➔ **OCCUPATION:** National security adviser, United States secretary of state, provost of Stanford University ➔ **BOLDEST MOMENT:** Breaking barriers with every new job title

Sandra Day O'CONNOR

LADY OF JUSTICE

On July 6, 1981, justice Sandra Day O'Connor was working in her office when her telephone rang. It was U.S. president Ronald Reagan, calling to tell her that he was planning to nominate her for a spot on the U.S. Supreme Court. O'Connor was highly qualified for the position: She had spent 15 years as a state senator in Arizona, U.S.A., and then as a judge on the state's most important courts. But still, she was shocked. No woman had ever served on the Supreme Court before.

She held the position for 24 years. Sometimes, the other justices would be split, with four voting one way and four another. O'Connor became known as the swing voter whose opinion often decided a case. She was regarded for thinking carefully and voting for what she deemed best upheld the U.S. Constitution. In one of her most famous cases, *Mississippi University for Women* v. *Hogan*, in 1982, she and the Court ruled that it was unconstitutional for a nursing school to refuse to admit male students.

O'Connor faced a range of challenges as a woman in a field made up of mostly men. When she graduated from law school in 1952, she called more than 40 law firms asking for an interview. All of them told her that they didn't hire women. And when she first began on the Supreme Court, there weren't even women's restrooms near the court-room! But O'Connor didn't let these obstacles stop her, paving the way for the female justices who would follow in her footsteps.

> "DO THE BEST YOU CAN IN EVERY TASK, NO MATTER HOW UNIMPORTANT IT MAY SEEM AT THE TIME."
> —SANDRA DAY O'CONNOR

FEARLESS FACTS

➜ **BORN:** March 26, 1930, El Paso, Texas, U.S.A. ➜ **OCCUPATION:** United States Supreme Court Justice
➜ **BOLDEST MOMENT:** Breaking new ground for women in America's highest court

MOMENT OF BRAVERY

With danger marching ever closer, would this first lady use precious minutes to save a piece of history?

THE SITUATION

In the summer of 1814, President James Madison was locked in a ferocious battle with the British. He was losing the fight; the redcoats were overtaking the American soldiers and advancing toward the capital. The streets of Washington, D.C., flooded with people fleeing ahead of enemy troops.

Just six miles (9.7 km) away, First Lady Dolley Madison stood her ground in the White House, refusing to leave her home. Determined not to show fear, the unshakable first lady even sent out invitations to a dinner party! But by then the city was deserted, and no one showed up. Still, Madison refused to make her escape—until she received a message from her husband telling her to evacuate right away. With British troops marching closer with every second, Madison was scrambling to leave when something caught her eye: a painting of the first American president, George Washington, hanging in the State Dining Room. Madison knew time was running out for her to get out of danger. But she also knew that if the enemy got their hands on the presidential portrait, they would destroy it.

THE MOMENT OF TRUTH

With her time to flee to safety ticking away, Madison chose to risk her own life for the painting. The artwork's frame was screwed to the wall, so she ordered servants to break it and take down the canvas inside. It was pulled out, rolled up, and hustled away by two friends who had come to the White House to offer their help. Only once Madison had ensured the painting was safe did she escape to safety.

THE LEGACY

Madison made it out, but British troops burned the White House soon after her escape. (It was reconstructed in 1817.) Had it not been for her act of courage, the painting would have burned with it. Today, the art the famous first lady risked everything to rescue is a national treasure and a priceless piece of history. It now hangs safely in the East Room of the White House.

CHAPTER TWO

Gritty GIRLS

We've heard it all before: Girls can't play sports as well as boys. Games are not exciting because females are not strong enough or fast enough—or just not good enough. Well, we're calling a foul on that idea. Want proof? Read on. This chapter is dedicated to the women who tear it up on the field and at the gym, track, pool, ice rink, and anywhere else they compete. The athletic heroines in this chapter prove that women have what it takes to win, even when the odds are against them. Get ready to be inspired to go the distance.

American skier Lindsey Vonn competes in Courchevel, France, in 2015.

Jackie JOYNER-KERSEE

SUPERWOMAN OF SPORTS

When Jackie Joyner-Kersee was born, her grandmother said, "Someday this girl will be the first lady of something." So her family named her after Jacqueline Kennedy, President John F. Kennedy's wife. Jackie's grandmother was right: Jackie became the first lady of track and field. Many people even consider her the greatest female athlete of all time.

RUNNING START

Jackie grew up in a rough part of East St. Louis, Illinois, U.S.A. Her family often didn't have enough money to heat their house or buy clothes for Jackie or her brother and two younger sisters. But Jackie was determined to make a better life for herself. She was already a top student and star athlete when, in 1976, she watched the Summer Olympics on television. Jackie dreamed that someday she would be one of the athletes competing for the gold. She threw herself into training as hard as she could. In high school, she excelled in volleyball and basketball, but her first love was track and field. During her junior year, she set the Illinois high school long jump record for women with a 21.92-foot (6.68-m) leap. At the age of 19, she began training seriously for the Olympics.

"IF A YOUNG FEMALE SEES MY DREAMS AND GOALS COME TRUE, THEY WILL REALIZE THEIR DREAMS AND GOALS MIGHT COME TRUE ALSO."
—JACKIE JOYNER-KERSEE

FEARLESS FACTS

➔ **BORN:** March 3, 1962, East St. Louis, Illinois, U.S.A. ➔ **OCCUPATION:** Track athlete
➔ **BOLDEST MOMENT:** Setting records that still stand today

Jackie's event was the heptathlon, an event that combines seven sports in one: a 100-meter (328-ft) hurdle race, the high jump, shot put, a 200-meter (656-ft) race, the long jump, the javelin throw, and, finally, an 800-meter (2,625-ft) race. The heptathlon tests speed, flexibility, precision, and raw strength—skills that, for most athletes, oppose one another. It's one of the toughest events in the Olympic Games.

SUPERWOMAN

In 1984, Joyner-Kersee headed to Los Angeles, California, U.S.A., to compete in her first Olympic Games. As she lined up for the final event, the 800-meter (2,625-foot) race, she was 31 points ahead of her closest rival, Australia's Glynis Nunn. Joyner-Kersee could lose to Nunn by 2.13 seconds and still win the gold. Unfortunately, fate had other plans: Hindered by a torn hamstring she'd suffered just two weeks before the event, she came in 2.46 seconds behind Nunn. Joyner-Kersee had lost the big race, but little did people know, she was just getting started.

Returning from the Olympics with a silver, Jackie Joyner-Kersee immediately began training for the 1988 Games in South Korea. Four years of hard work paid off—this time, she took gold in the heptathlon. *Sports Illustrated* magazine put her photo on the cover with the title "Super Woman," a name she lived up to. Joyner-Kersee would go on to win three golds, a silver, and two bronzes in the heptathlon and long jump—the most medals of any woman in Olympic track and field history. She still holds the world record for the heptathlon today—and the next five highest scores, too.

Through all of her success, Joyner-Kersee battled asthma, a disease that causes wheezing, shortness of breath, and coughing. Exercise made her condition worse, but Jackie didn't let it slow her down. She retired from the track at age 38. Today she is devoted to sharing the positive influence of athletics with others. Inspired by the closing of her neighborhood community center, she opened the Jackie Joyner-Kersee Foundation in East St. Louis in 1995 to give kids a safe place in the community to play sports, take classes, and develop leadership skills.

Jackie Joyner-Kersee crosses the finish line at a track event in 1985 (right) and clears the high jump bar during the U.S. Olympic Trials in 1988 (below).

AMERICA'S FIRST OLYMPIC HERO: Jesse Owens (1913–1980)

DARING DUDE

The eyes of the world were on Jesse Owens at the 1936 Olympic Games in Berlin, Germany—and not just because he was a record-setting athlete with a winning personality. Held in Germany under Adolf Hitler's Nazi regime, these Summer Games were about more than the thrill of international competition. The Nazi party believed in a poisonous myth: that Jewish and black people were inferior. These games were the Nazis' opportunity to showcase the supposed superiority of Germany's Aryan "race," and Hitler was certain his nation's athletes would dominate every event. Jesse Owens, the black grandson of slaves, proved him very wrong. With Hitler watching from the stands, Owens earned four gold track and field medals. Won over by his sportsmanship, German spectators chanted his name. For the Nazis, Owens's triumph was a defeat.

LADY LEGENDS OF SPORTS

ATHLETIC ICONS

From the world's fastest woman to the one who found no sport too tough, the women on these pages are true athletic icons. They not only left lasting marks on their sport but also shattered stereotypes of what women can do. Some are living legends; all will never be forgotten.

MOST MEDALED: Larisa Latynina (1934–)

Ukrainian-born Larisa Latynina started out training to be a dancer. When her ballet studio closed, she looked for an outlet for her athletic talent and competitive drive and found one in gymnastics. As a gymnast, she won 18 Olympic medals, and half of them were gold. Latynina held her medal record for nearly 50 years, until swimmer Michael Phelps broke it at the 2012 Olympic Games in London. Latynina was there in the stands, applauding Phelps as he won his 19th medal.

FASTEST WOMAN IN THE WORLD: Florence Griffith Joyner (1959–1998)

In 1988, American athlete Florence Griffith Joyner (sister-in-law of Jackie Joyner-Kersee) set a world record for the 100-meter (328-foot) race during the Olympic Trials quarterfinals, crossing the finish line in a blazingly fast 10.49 seconds. Then, she set another world record, for the 200-meter (656-foot) race, at the 1988 Olympic Games in Seoul, South Korea. Those times still stand today, and no other athlete has even come close to matching them. Joyner broke records with flair, often showing up to the track sporting one-legged body suits and six-inch (1.5-cm)-long fingernails. But it was her fleet feet that earned her a place in the history books: Flo-Jo is considered the fastest woman of all time.

CHAMPION ON ICE: Surya Bonaly (1973–)

French-American champion figure skater Surya Bonaly was famous for her trademark backflip; she is the only skater—man or woman—in history to ever land it on one foot. Though this move wasn't allowed in Olympic competition, Bonaly did it anyway in the 1998 games, shocking the crowd and judges with her boldness—and her show-stopping athleticism. The move is illegal to this day, and no other skater has ever attempted it. Though figure skating's color barrier was incredibly tough to crack (it wasn't until 1997 that the first African-American woman—Mabel Fairbanks—was inducted into the U.S. Figure Skating Hall of Fame), Bonaly rose to the top tier of the sport—and she did it on her own terms. Besides shaking up the figure skating world with her rebellious performances, Bonaly also famously bucked the female figure skater's dress code by not wearing tights and by choosing glitzy costumes in bright colors instead of more traditional colors or pastels.

ALL-AROUND ATHLETE: Babe Didrikson Zaharias (1911–1956)

When Babe was growing up in Texas, U.S.A., she took up every sport she could—and excelled at them all. Asked if there was anything she didn't play, she said, "Yeah, dolls." After reading about the 1928 Olympics in her father's newspapers, she decided she would compete one day. She started training for track and field by jumping over hedges in her neighborhood. Four years later, at the 1932 Olympics, Zaharias won medals in the hurdles, high jump, and javelin throw. Looking for a new challenge, she took up golf. She became America's first female golf celebrity, dominating the sport in the 1940s and early 1950s, and winning 99 tournaments in her professional career. The Associated Press news organization voted her Female Athlete of the Year six times.

HIS ROYAL AIRNESS: Michael Jordan (1963–)

DARING DUDE

He led the Chicago Bulls to win six championships and took home eight MVP awards, but Michael Jordan is considered the world's greatest basketball player for more than just his stats. Jordan turned every throw into an air show. He soared toward the basket, defying the laws of physics, seeming to change direction in midair. Jordan's opponents on the court envied his skills. Fans idolized him. Everyone wanted to be "like Mike." After leading the Bulls to a three-peat—winning three consecutive championships—Jordan took time out to play professional baseball. He returned to the court in 1995 and helped the Bulls score another three-peat before retiring in 1999.

Venus & Serena WILLIAMS

TWICE THE POWER

Venus Williams

> "IT DOESN'T MATTER WHAT YOUR BACKGROUND IS AND WHERE YOU COME FROM, IF YOU HAVE DREAMS AND GOALS, THAT'S ALL THAT MATTERS."
> —SERENA WILLIAMS

Serena Williams

Venus and Serena Williams grew up in the tough neighborhood of Compton, Los Angeles. Their tennis courts had potholes, and their rackets were shabby. Tennis was a sport dominated by wealthy white people. But the sisters played anyway, starting when they were just four years old. They practiced six hours a day with their father, who coached neighborhood kids after learning the sport himself from books and instructional videos.

The girls had a natural ability for the sport from the get-go. Serena won her first tennis competition at age four and, along with her sister, just kept getting better. Both girls turned professional at age 14. Both have won numerous Grand Slam titles and doubles competitions, and each sister has been ranked number one in the world at some point in her career.

Venus has the fastest serve in women's tennis; she can send the ball speeding over the net at 129 miles an hour (208 km/h)! She was the first black woman to ever be ranked number one in tennis. Serena has an incredibly powerful forehand shot and a serve just 0.4 mile an hour (0.6 km/h) slower than her sister's. Serena is often referred to as the greatest female player of all time.

Together, the Williams sisters have changed the sport of tennis. They have broken down color barriers and made the sport more accessible to people from all walks of life. And their powerful style of play has brought a new level of athleticism to women's tennis.

FEARLESS FACTS

➲ **BORN:** June 17, 1980, Lynwood, California, U.S.A., and September 26, 1981, Saginaw, Michigan, U.S.A.
➲ **OCCUPATION:** Tennis players ➲ **BOLDEST MOMENT:** Serving up a new era of women's tennis

Misty MAY-TREANOR & Kerri WALSH JENNINGS

THE DREAM TEAM

On August 8, 2012, in London, England, Misty May-Treanor and Kerri Walsh Jennings danced on the sand. They had just completed their third Olympic Games as teammates—and won their third gold medal.

Growing up, Kerri and Misty played against each other on opposing high school teams at a time when beach volleyball wasn't yet an Olympic sport. But they didn't meet until Kerri asked Misty—a star player who had taken her high school indoor volleyball team to two state championships—to autograph a towel. They started playing together after college and clicked right away.

May-Treanor and Jennings aren't just teammates, they're best friends who have stayed close and supported each other through their 11 years as partners on the court. After 2008, May-Treanor had to take a break from volleyball because she injured her Achilles tendon. Jennings took a hiatus, too, and had kids. But even though their playing took a time-out, their friendship didn't. The two came back to win the gold in London in 2012.

Across their three trips to the Olympics (in 2004, 2008, and 2012), they played 43 sets and lost only once. The dream team won three gold medals in a row, the first women's beach volleyball team in Olympic history to accomplish that feat. Their third gold medal clinched their spot on many lists as the best beach volleyball team ever—male or female.

"I DON'T HAVE A SISTER BUT I CONSIDER HER A SISTER. WE'VE BEEN THROUGH THICK AND THIN."
—MISTY MAY-TREANOR

Misty May-Treanor (left) and Kerri Walsh Jennings (right)

FEARLESS FACTS

➲ **BORN:** July 30, 1977, Los Angeles, California, U.S.A., and August 15, 1978, Santa Clara, California, U.S.A. ➲ **OCCUPATION:** Beach volleyball players ➲ **BOLDEST MOMENT:** Spiking their way to three Olympic victories

WOMEN TO WATCH
TODAY'S SUPERSTARS

These young athletes may have big challenges ahead, but that's not slowing them down. Keep your eyes open for them in the headlines, because this won't be the last time you read their names. From ski racers to swimmers to ballerinas, these women are legends in the making ... and they're already changing sports history.

SWIMMING'S NEXT SUPERSTAR:
Katie Ledecky (1997–)

"Set goals that, when you set them, you think they're impossible," says champion swimmer Katie Ledecky. Wise words from a gutsy gal who—at just 15 years old—was the youngest athlete to compete at the 2012 Olympic Games. She entered only one event— the 800-meter freestyle—and she won it handily.

Since then, Ledecky has become the most dominant freestyle swimmer—male or female—on Earth, breaking ten world records. At the 2015 FINA World Championships in Kazan, Russia, she became the first woman to win four individual gold medals at a world championship and the first swimmer in history to sweep the 200-, 400-, 800-, and 1,500-meter freestyle events, a feat now nicknamed a Ledecky slam. For a swimmer to be so good at a mix of sprint and endurance races is almost unheard of. Ledecky is predicted to take the world by storm at the 2016 Olympics in Rio de Janeiro, Brazil.

SPEED RACER: Lindsey Vonn (1984–)

The only American woman ever to win a gold medal for downhill skiing, Lindsey Vonn is considered by many to be the top female skier in the world. She has flown downhill at speeds exceeding 84 miles an hour (135 km/h)—faster than you are legally allowed to drive down most highways! But she wasn't born with athletic talent. Growing up in Burnsville, Minnesota, U.S.A., she had a hard time with figure skating and was just average on the soccer field. It's her

DANCING FEET: Misty Copeland
(1982–)

Most ballerinas grow up dancing, but Misty Copeland didn't begin until age 13, when her Los Angeles, California, U.S.A., middle school drill team coach saw her talent and encouraged her to take ballet classes at the local Boys & Girls Club. She didn't look like the other dancers and was often told she was too muscular and too short. But in 1999 this unlikely ballerina was invited to join the famous American Ballet Theater in New York City where, for 10 years, she was the only African-American ballerina. Despite her obstacles, Copeland has pirouetted her way to the top—and changed the world's mind about what a dancer is supposed to look like: In 2015 she became the first African-American woman to be named a principal dancer—the highest level—in the 75-year history of the American Ballet Theater.

"You can do anything you want, even if you are being told negative things," Copeland says. "Stay strong and find motivation."

WILD RIDER: Robbie Maddison (1981–)

DARING DUDE

This Australian motocross star makes the impossible look … well, still impossible! Maddison (aka Maddo) doesn't just leap landmarks—from Greek canals to football stadiums—he often performs outrageous tricks in the process: He even did a backflip while leaping over the opened Tower Bridge, in London, England! Maddo—who's held world records for longest distance jumped on a motorcycle—even managed to surf a dangerous monster wave in Tahiti while riding a motorcycle equipped with skis. Some consider him a modern-day Evel Knievel, the legendary landmark-leaping daredevil of the 1970s.

But does he ever get hurt? You bet! "In some ways, serious injuries helped me refocus on how important this whole adventure around the world is to me," he says. "It fires me up more than ever, so it's a blessing in disguise."

determination that has made Vonn a champion: She spends as many as seven hours in the gym every day, six days a week.

Ski racing is exciting but dangerous: In 2013, after experiencing some heavy crashes on the slopes that required knee surgery and months of rehabilitation, Vonn tore two ligaments and fractured her knee, and she had to sit out the 2014 Olympics. But she refused to be discouraged and vowed to come back better than ever. In 2015, with her 63rd victory, Vonn became the winningest woman in World Cup history.

Battle OF THE

BILLIE JEAN KING

Billie Jean was 29 years old and already a star player with ten singles championships under her belt when Bobby Riggs challenged her to what would become a pivotal moment in her career and in sports history. At first, she refused to take Riggs's bait. But Riggs goaded her, boasting that women were inferior to men and couldn't handle the pressure of the game. It was the 1970s, a time when many people shared Riggs's sexist attitude and regarded women as lesser than men. King knew that if she could win, she could prove to the world that Riggs was wrong. She wanted to put Riggs in his place on behalf of women everywhere. So King accepted the challenge, and on September 20, 1973, she met Riggs on the court.

VS.

SEXES

THE CROWD

More than 30,000 fans crowded the Houston Astrodome in Texas, U.S.A., to see the Battle of the Sexes, and 90 million more tuned in to see the match on television. The eyes of the world were watching to see who would prevail.

THE MATCH

King's strategy was to tire out her bigger, stronger opponent, who was almost twice her age and who hadn't been practicing. It was a smart play. She won the first set 6-4, and the second set 6-3. Then, it was set three. The score was 5-3, in favor of King. One more point and the match was hers. Riggs brought his racket up to volley, and … hit the ball into the net. King threw her racket into the air in celebration. Riggs gathered the energy to hop the net and whispered in King's ear, "I underestimated you." King's victory in the Battle of the Sexes proved that women athletes could beat men, fair and square.

THE AFTERMATH

King became a celebrity overnight. She landed endorsement deals for products like Nike sneakers and Colgate toothpaste—common for top female athletes today but unheard of at the time. The following year, she reportedly earned nearly $1 million from product endorsements and tournament winnings, paving the way for other top-earning female superstar athletes. She founded *WomenSports* magazine and started the Women's Sports Foundation, an organization devoted to giving female athletes more opportunities. Today, she is honored as a pioneer of women in sports.

BOBBY RIGGS

Bobby Riggs was once considered one of the best tennis players in the world. He won the men's singles, doubles, and mixed doubles at Wimbledon in 1939, before retiring from the sport in 1951. But in 1973, at age 55, Riggs wanted to get back in the spotlight. He announced that he thought he could still beat any female player in the world and challenged the No. 1-ranked woman, Margaret Court, to a match. Riggs beat her so badly the game was nicknamed the Mother's Day Massacre. Next, Riggs challenged Billie Jean King.

World Cup WARRIORS

THE MOST FAMOUS TEAM IN WOMEN'S SPORTS HISTORY

In the 1990s, few people in America cared about soccer. Even fewer cared about women's soccer: Many people didn't even know the United States had a team! But one tough and talented group of women was about to change that.

TEAM SPIRIT

On her own, each woman was a star player. There was talented defender Brandi Chastain, expert header Michelle Akers, daring goalie Briana Scurry, and star forward Mia Hamm—still considered by many to be the best in history. But it was the group's camaraderie that made them a great team. They danced on the bus, ate peanut butter and jelly sandwiches when their team money ran low, and even took baths in the hotel pool when one of their tournament stops didn't have electricity or running water. America fell in love with this gutsy, fun-loving, and talented team.

THE WORLD CUP

The teammates' hearts were pounding as they waited in the locker room for their first match of the 1999 World Cup, against Denmark. They were playing in professional stadiums much bigger than what they were used to—what if their games didn't sell enough tickets to fill them? They didn't need to worry. As they filed onto the field, nearly 79,000 screaming fans greeted them.

"WE WANTED IT TO GO WELL, AND NOT JUST FOR US BUT FOR THE FUTURE OF ALL OF WOMEN'S SPORT."
—BRANDI CHASTAIN

FEARLESS FACTS

➔ **OCCUPATION:** Soccer team   ➔ **BOLDEST MOMENT:** Putting women's soccer on the map

Members of the U.S. Women's National Team celebrate winning the 1999 FIFA Women's World Cup (above); player Brandi Chastain reacts after kicking in the game-winning penalty shootout goal (right).

The game went into overtime, then into a shoot-out—when players from each team take turns facing the goalie one-on-one. It came down to the last shooter, Chastain. Her teammates behind her, she flew toward the net. Trying to fake out the goalie, she reached out with her weaker left foot and kicked. The ball hit the net. GOOOAALL! The crowd exploded. Chastain collapsed to her knees and ripped off her jersey in cele-bration. The girls jumped on each other, screaming with joy. They had done it.

By giving the sport and each other their all, this group of women showed the millions of girls watching them on TV and in the stands that teamwork and perseverance can take you all the way to your goal.

The U.S. team beat Denmark, then Nigeria, then North Korea. Fans mobbed them for their autographs, and their faces were in every newspaper. America loved them.

All was going well until the match against Germany. Five minutes in, Brandi Chastain tried to pass the ball—and it accidentally went into her own team's net. She was crushed, and the U.S. lost momentum. By halftime, they were down a goal. But the team didn't blame Chastain, even though she had made a terrible mistake that could have cost them the game. With their support behind her, she came back to slam the ball into Germany's net. After scoring one more goal, the U.S. was on to the semifinals, then the final game. They would face off against China. At that time, the Chinese were the best team in the world. The American women were the underdogs.

THE BIG GAME

From the second the clock started at the final World Cup game on July 10, 1999, in Pasadena, California, U.S.A., the match was a nail-biter. Over and over, the Americans would get the ball, and the Chinese would kick it away. The Americans were exhausted. But they refused to give up. They knew their opponents were tired, too. If they could be the tougher team, they would win.

MOUNTAIN MEN: DARING DUDE
Tommy Caldwell (1978–) and Kevin Jorgeson (1984–)

Talk about teamwork taking you all the way to the top! After nearly three weeks of hanging from a sheer mountainside, their fingertips ban-daged and bleeding, this dynamic climbing duo reached the summit of El Capitan in California's Yosemite National Park in 2015. They weren't the first men to scramble up the Dawn Wall—consid-ered one of the climbing world's most treacherous routes—but they were the first to free-climb it: using only their fingertips and feet to wedge into crevices and grip narrow ledges. (Free climbers still wear harnesses and ropes as a safety precaution.) The team had prac-ticed for five years and failed in previous attempts, but they always stuck together through good climbs and bad. When Jorgeson got stymied by a tricky stretch of wall for ten days, Caldwell waited and offered encouragement from their dangling tent (called a portaledge). They persevered, and they got to the top together.

NO GIRLS ALLOWED

THEY DID IT ANYWAY!

Some sports have long been considered the territory of men—and men only. Women were too weak to send a golf ball flying hundreds of yards, too dainty to muscle a slap-shot into a hockey net. But nobody told these gutsy gals. They proved that women can compete with—and beat—the boys.

ICE QUEEN: Manon Rhéaume (1972–)

On September 23, 1992, Manon Rhéaume went where no woman had gone before: onto the ice to play in a professional hockey game. Rhéaume had been playing goalie in Canada's junior leagues since she was five years old. She was ready. She stopped seven of the nine shots she faced for the Tampa Bay Lightning in its preseason game against the St. Louis Blues (both in the U.S.A.). She went on to play for eight different men's minor league teams in four minor leagues, and win two World Championship gold medals and an Olympic silver medal for Canada. And she changed hockey forever by showing that a woman could face off with the men. She's a role model for women hockey players everywhere—several of whom have followed in her footsteps and joined men's teams. Today, Rhéaume coaches young girls in the sport, as well as her two hockey-player sons.

BELLE OF THE BALL: Ann Meyers Drysdale (1955–)

Ann Meyers Drysdale was a basketball phenomenon. Crowds loved it when Ann—the first woman ever signed to a four-year athletic scholarship to the University of California, Los Angeles—took the women's team to a championship in her senior year of college. But then she did something that many people at the time didn't like. Drysdale wanted to play with the best, and she had the talent to do it, so she tried out for the Indiana Pacers, a team in the all-men's National Basketball Association (NBA). She was the first—and only—woman ever to attempt the feat. Drysdale didn't make the team, but she did make history. She went on to break more barriers, among them becoming the only female vice president in the National Basketball Association.

GUTSY GOLFER: Annika Sörenstam (1970–)

Sometimes called the Tiger Woods of women's golf, this Swedish superstar was almost unbeatable on the course. But she didn't start out that way: When Sörenstam took up the sport at age 12, she was so shy that she would sometimes lose on purpose to avoid speaking to anyone after a win. Her will to succeed eventually beat out her bashful nature, and today she holds the record as the only woman in history to have completed a professional golf game in under 60 strokes. But being the best female golfer in the world wasn't enough for Sörenstam. She wanted to compete against men, and she did. Sörenstam was invited to play in the Bank of America Colonial golf tournament on May 22, 2003, making her the first woman to play in the Professional Golfers' Association (PGA) tour event since Babe Didrikson Zaharias.

FULL THROTTLE: Janet Guthrie (1938–)

After she graduated from the University of Michigan in Ann Arbor, U.S.A., with a degree in physics, Janet Guthrie took a job as an aerospace engineer. But then she changed tracks ... to be a race car driver. In 1976, she became the first woman to race in the Indianapolis 500, one of the biggest automobile races in the world. That year, she came in 29th, but a year later, she finished ninth in that race. Her record stood until 2005, when female race car star Danica Patrick took it a step further and came in fourth. Today, Guthrie's helmet and driver's suit are at the world-renowned Smithsonian Institution in Washington, D.C.

HORSEPLAY: Julie Krone (1963–)

By the time she was 13, Julie Krone knew what her life goal was: to become the best jockey in the world, in the most dangerous sport there is. All jockeys are on the shorter side, but Krone stands just four feet eleven inches (1.5 m) tall, with a high-pitched voice that got her ridiculed in high school. But she was much tougher than she looked. During her career, she was smacked, bumped, knocked off her horse, and trampled ... but she always got back in the saddle. She won more than 3,700 races, making her the winning-est female jockey of all time. And in 1993, she became the first woman to win in one of the races of the Triple Crown—the most famous event in horse racing.

Pat SUMMITT

LEGENDARY HEAD COACH

When Pat Summitt was 22, she was hired to be the assistant coach of the women's basketball team at the University of Tennessee, U.S.A. A few weeks later, the head coach quit, and it was suddenly Summitt's job to lead the team. She had never coached a game in her life.

Even though, at the time, the women's basketball team didn't have a big audience, Summitt devoted herself completely to her new position. She even swept the floors, set out chairs, washed the uniforms, and drove the team to games in a van. After work, she went to school to get her master's degree in physical education. And on the side, Summitt—a player herself—trained as part of Team U.S.A. for the 1976 Olympics—the first one that included women's basketball. She won a silver medal.

Four months later, in her third year of coaching, she coached her team—the Lady Vols—to the NCAA (National Collegiate Athletic Association) championships. Summitt was known for demanding the very best of her players—and it worked. The Lady Vols went on to eight national championships, and the players became superstars of women's basketball.

Summitt also coached the gold medal–winning women's U.S. basketball team at the 1984 Olympics. In 2000, she was inducted into the Basketball Hall of Fame and named the Naismith Coach of the Century. She is considered one of the best coaches—male or female—in the history of sports.

> "TEAMWORK IS WHAT MAKES UNCOMMON PEOPLE CAPABLE OF ACHIEVING UNCOMMON RESULTS."
> —PAT SUMMITT

FEARLESS FACTS

➔ **BORN:** June 14, 1952, Clarksville, Tennessee, U.S.A. ➔ **OCCUPATION:** Head coach
➔ **BOLDEST MOMENT:** Leading her team to victory

Linda COHN

VOICE OF THE GAME

Linda Cohn knew she wanted to be a sports broadcaster when she was in college. But there was a problem: There were only a couple of female sportscasters. Could Cohn make it when so many women before her hadn't?

It was a good thing Cohn already knew something about being the only girl in her field. In high school, she had tried out for—and won—a spot on the boys' hockey team as a goalie. "It sure beat the senior prom," she joked. In 1987, she landed a position as the first woman sports anchor on a national radio network. Soon after, she got in front of the cameras as a sportscaster. And in 1992, she was hired as an anchor for ESPN's *SportsCenter*. She remains an anchor for ESPN today.

Cohn is a sports fanatic, and it shows when she speaks about her favorite teams. Viewers love her passion; it's one of the reasons she is so successful in her job. But it wasn't easy for her to get there. When she first started at ESPN, her boss told her, "Most of the women before you have failed here." Cohn refused to be one of them. She believed that as long as she knew her stuff, she would be a great sportscaster. And she was right. On Sunday, February 21, 2016, Cohn anchored her 5,000th *SportsCenter* episode—more than anyone else in history.

Today, more women than ever are entering the field—like ex-basketball star Ann Meyers Drysdale, who was the first woman to ever broadcast an NBA game. Cohn's mastery of the mic helped make that possible.

> "I'M ALWAYS THINKING 'HOW CAN I CONTINUE TO GROW?'"
> —LINDA COHN

FEARLESS FACTS

➜ **BORN:** November 10, 1959, Long Island, New York, U.S.A. ➜ **OCCUPATION:** Sports anchor
➜ **BOLDEST MOMENT:** Speaking up for women in sportscasting

MOMENT OF BRAVERY

When this polo pioneer rode into a roadblock, she didn't give up. Could she find a way around it—and change her sport forever?

THE SITUATION

Growing up near the polo fields at a country club in Los Angeles, California, Sue Sally Hale would watch the players expertly swing their long mallets as they thundered down the field on sleek horses. Hale wanted to be part of the thrill—and as a natural-born horsewoman who had ridden her first pony at age three, she had the chops to do it. But when she asked about joining in, she found out something crushing: Women weren't allowed to play.

That would be enough to make most people shrug and look for another sport. But it didn't stop Hale.

THE MOMENT OF TRUTH

Hale pulled on an oversized shirt, stuffed her hair up under her helmet, and used a tube of mascara to draw a mustache on her lip. Then, she trotted off to the polo fields and signed up to compete under the name A. Jones.

Amazingly, her scheme worked. Hale kept up her false identity for 20 years. After matches, she would rush back to her trailer, remove her disguise, and head to the post-game party. She got a kick out of hearing people praising a certain mysterious player who had disappeared from the field as soon as the match ended. At first, only her teammates knew the truth. Eventually, the word got out that the man in the mustache was really Hale.

THE LEGACY

Hale tried over and over to get the U.S. Polo Association to change its rules and allow her to play under her true name. Finally, her friends in the polo world got involved, threatening to embarrass the association by revealing that it had been letting a woman into its tournaments for two decades. In 1972, the U.S. Polo Association admitted Hale as the first female in the sport. She never stopped challenging polo's rules and continually pushed for more female players to be allowed. Today, the U.S. Polo Association counts hundreds of women among its members, including Hale's daughter, Sunny. They owe their spots in the sport to Hale's fake mustache—and her very real bravery.

CHAPTER THREE

Heroines ON THE JOB

Not all heroines strive to rule nations or take home the gold. Sometimes, women are at their best and bravest when simply doing their jobs. From women who battled bad guys to gals who proved they could be business bosses, these workplace warriors went head-to-head with fearsome forces and got the job done—no matter what it took.

Colonel Jeannie Leavitt of the U.S. Air Force signals her crew chief before taking off at Seymour Johnson Air Force Base in North Carolina, U.S.A., in 2013.

Mavis BATEY

AND THE CODE BREAKERS OF BLETCHLEY PARK

THE ENIGMA MACHINE PUT SECRET MESSAGES INTO A CODE MANY THOUGHT WAS UNBREAKABLE.

The heroes of World War II weren't all fighters on the front lines. Far away from the action in an English countryside estate called Bletchley Park, a group of people worked in secret. They were code breakers: Their job was to decipher encrypted, top secret Nazi communications and use what they learned to help defeat Hitler's army. Nearly 10,000 people worked at Bletchley. They told no one what they were doing there—not even their families. They weren't showered with medals or honored with parades, but they were heroes all the same. Without the Bletchley code breakers, historians estimate, the war would have lasted two to four years longer. They were mathematicians, linguists, and crossword puzzle experts—and more than two-thirds of them were women. One was named Mavis Batey.

WOMAN VS. MACHINE

Batey was a British college student studying German when World War II broke out. She volunteered to be a nurse, but the army had other ideas. Batey was recruited to hunt for hidden messages in German newspapers and then, having done well, she was sent to Bletchley to match wits against the Enigma machine, a Nazi coding device so sophisticated that some thought it would be impossible to crack.

FEARLESS FACTS

➔ **BORN:** May 5, 1921, Dulwich, London, England ➔ **DIED:** November 12, 2013, West Sussex, England ➔ **OCCUPATION:** Code breaker ➔ **BOLDEST MOMENT:** Cracking secret messages and helping win World War II

Resembling an oversize typewriter, the Enigma machine didn't look very intimidating—but it was a formidable foe. Its series of spinning electric rotors were mind-bogglingly good at scrambling messages. They could make each letter appear in more than 150 trillion different ways. Some of Britain's brightest minds had tried to figure out how the Enigma worked—and failed.

Batey was only 19 when she went to work trying to crack Enigma messages from the Italian Navy, part of the enemy Axis that also included Germany and Japan. One day in late March 1941, Batey accomplished a small victory—she managed to decode an ominous transmission that read, "Today's the day minus three." That meant Batey had just three days to find out what the Italian Navy was planning to do. If she couldn't, British soldiers might lose their lives.

Batey and her team had worked day and night for nearly three days when they finally cracked another message. It told them where and when the Italian Navy was planning to launch an attack against British ships. The code breakers rushed the message to the British Navy, which launched a preemptive strike that left the enemy fleet crippled for the rest of the war.

SPY SECRETS

With the code breakers' help, the Allies—the side fighting the Nazis, which included Britain and the United States—launched a top secret operation called XX, or Double-Cross, which used captured Nazi spies to send false messages to the enemy. The Allies used XX to pass the Germans a phony location for the famous D-Day invasion of June 6, 1944, convincing them it would happen at the beach of Pas-de-Calais, France, instead of its actual location 180 miles (290 km) away in Normandy. The surprise attack helped turn the tide and win the war.

Even once the war was over, Batey and the other code breakers at Bletchley had to keep their work a secret. Batey's three children grew up never knowing about their mother's wartime work. It wasn't until the 1970s that the story of Bletchley Park—and its squad of code breaking heroines—was revealed to the world.

Female code breakers at Bletchley Park pose for a rare photo.

MASTERMINDS:
More Female Code Breakers of Bletchley Park

JOAN CLARKE

Joan Clarke started out as a secretary and quickly proved her talent. She was soon put to work breaking coded messages about Nazi submarines that were hunting down Allied ships. It was one of the most difficult jobs at Bletchley. Clarke went on to a career in code breaking after the war, one of the few women at Bletchley Park to do so.

MARGARET BULLEN

Margaret Bullen was working for a bank until she one day received a mysterious message from the British military asking her to travel to London for an interview. Bullen aced the interview and went to work at Bletchley Park, where she helped build two early computers. One of them, called the Colossus, was designed to speed up the decoding of coded German radio messages. It was the world's first digital electronic computer.

MARGARET ROCK

A talented mathematician, Margaret Rock worked with Mavis Batey to decode messages that allowed the Allies to gain control of the German spy network. Code breaker Dilly Knox, who led the all-female team, gave Rock and Batey all the credit for their feat.

IN THE LINE OF DUTY
ALL IN A DAY'S WORK

Once upon a time, people thought some jobs were just too dangerous for delicate ladies ... until these women proved they were no damsels in distress. From the first woman in history to wear a police officer's badge to the first female to pilot a fighter jet, these pioneering heroines found no task too tough.

HEROINE OF 9/11: Lt. Brenda Berkman (1951–)

When the New York City Fire Department began allowing women to test for firefighter positions, in 1977, lawyer Brenda Berkman fought in court to challenge the fairness of the physical test they had to pass. When she won a discrimination lawsuit that truly opened the doors for female firefighters for the first time, Berkman was one of the first to join their ranks. But little did she know that was not the biggest challenge she would face in her career. Berkman was off duty when the first plane hit the World Trade Center on September 11, 2001. She threw on her uniform and ran to the scene without a second thought. She was a leader among the female firefighters of New York City—just 25 women among 11,500 men. After the attacks, Berkman worked for 48 hours straight. She walked across rubble seven stories high and dug through debris until her hands bled. But Berkman had fought to have the job she loved, and when her city needed her most, she was there.

FIRST FEMALE FIREFIGHTER: Molly Williams
(ca 1800–?)

Brenda Berkman was a pioneer, but she wasn't the first known female firefighter—that title goes to Molly Williams, who took up the hose nearly 200 years before her. Williams was a slave in New York City who became a member of the Oceanus Engine Company No. 11 in 1815. She fought fires while wearing a dress and apron, but she was as tough as the male firefighters, once dragging the water pumper during a blizzard to reach the site of a fire.

FIRST FEMALE FIGHTER PILOT:
Col. Jeannie Leavitt (1967–)

Even once women were officially permitted to join the military—as nurses during the last two years of World War I—it was another 76 years before they were allowed to fight in combat. Many military leaders thought they weren't up to the job. In 1991, a retired U.S. Marine Corps general testified before Congress in protest of an amendment that would allow women pilots to fly combat positions. He said, "If you want to make a combat unit ineffective, add some women to it." But that attitude didn't stop Jeannie Leavitt. In 1993, the government forced the military to allow women to fly in combat, and Leavitt was the first woman to take advantage of these new rules. She started training to fly fighter jets and, in 1994, became the U.S. Air Force's first female fighter pilot. In May 2012, she became the first female commander of one of the largest combat fighter wings in the U.S. Air Force.

FIRST POLICEWOMAN:
Alice Stebbins Wells (1873–1957)

In the early 20th century, there were almost no women in law enforcement in the U.S. The few females on the police force weren't officers; they were matrons who cared for female prisoners. Los Angeles social worker Alice Stebbins Wells successfully petitioned her city government to change the rules and, in 1910, she became a Los Angeles Police Department (LAPD) officer and the nation's first policewoman. Wells, who hand-stitched her own uniform, received a special badge from the LAPD that read "Policewoman's Badge Number One." Throughout her career, Wells visited cities nationwide to encourage other women to join the police force. She argued that women officers were better suited than men for working with juvenile and female criminals. Two years after Stebbins got her badge, two other female officers were sworn in. By 1937, the LAPD employed 39 policewomen. Wells, who retired in 1940 after 30 years on the force, saw her work change law enforcement forever.

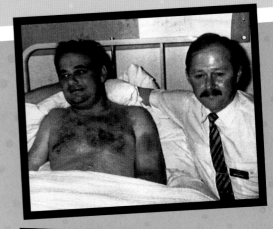

STRONG-ARM TACTICS:
Nigel Ogden

DARING DUDE

British Airways Flight 5390 had climbed just past 17,000 feet (5,182 m) into clear skies in June 1990 when the unthinkable happened: A panel of the cockpit's windshield blew loose in an explosion of mist and frigid wind. The sudden loss of pressure sucked the pilot from his seat and almost completely out the window. Flight attendant Nigel Ogden grabbed the pilot by his belt and held him in place as long as he could, with other crew members assisting throughout the terrifying ordeal. The copilot managed to land the plane safely. The pilot survived with some arm fractures and a broken thumb. Ogden suffered a dislocated shoulder and some frostbite from the freezing air but was otherwise physically unhurt.

Megan COFFEE

DEVOTED DOCTOR

On January 12, 2010, a violent earthquake struck 15 miles (25 km) southwest of Port-au-Prince, the capital of Haiti. The 7.0 earthquake and its two aftershocks devastated the city. Haiti's buildings—which weren't constructed to withstand the stress—collapsed, killing or trapping people inside. More than one million people were left homeless, and unsanitary conditions in ravaged towns enabled diseases to spread fast. There weren't enough doctors and nurses to treat the victims of the disaster.

Dr. Megan Coffee knew she could use her medical training to help. She flew to Haiti soon after the earthquake and was one of hundreds of doctors who made the trip to help strangers far from home. She spoke with nurses who told her that one of their most pressing issues was an outbreak of tuberculosis, a disease that spreads through the air when infected people cough and sneeze. Tuberculosis can be very dangerous if not treated properly.

Dr. Coffee set up a tuberculosis tent, treating 60 patients at a time. And she has since done whatever is needed to help her patients heal, from personally preparing pots of spaghetti to brainstorming ways to pay for medical supplies that her patients can't afford. In 2012, she raised more than $300,000 to support her tuberculosis tent.

Dr. Coffee doesn't collect a salary for her hard work; donations pay for her food and housing. She plans to stay in Haiti until her tuberculosis ward can run without her—no matter how long that takes.

> "I AM NOT PLANNING ON LEAVING THIS PROJECT. I JUST WANT IT TO BE MORE SUSTAINABLE."
> —MEGAN COFFEE

FEARLESS FACTS

➔ **BORN:** 1979, New York, New York, U.S.A.   ➔ **OCCUPATION:** Doctor of infectious disease
➔ **BOLDEST MOMENT:** Leaving her life behind to help earthquake victims in Haiti

Lisa LING

GUTSY JOURNALIST

When she was 16 years old, Lisa Ling auditioned to host the teen TV show *Scratch*, filmed in Sacramento, California, U.S.A. She got the spot, and she's never looked back. By age 18, she had become one of the youngest reporters for Channel One News, a network that played in middle school and high school classrooms across the country.

By age 25, Ling had become Channel One's senior war correspondent. Her work took her to more than 30 countries—many of them among the most dangerous places in the world. She put herself at great risk to report her stories, traveling to the jungles of Colombia to find labs that were making illegal drugs, covering the civil war in Algeria, and investigating a Russian company accused of smuggling nuclear weapons.

In 2005, Ling became the host of National Geographic's *Explorer* series—the first woman to hold the position in the show's 20-year history. By then, Ling was no stranger to danger, and she fearlessly traveled the world to investigate the looting of priceless artifacts in war-torn Iraq and the perilous world of American prisons. She even stepped into a submarine to journey more than 1,600 feet (488 m) to the bottom of the ocean to search for gold treasure.

Though her job puts her at risk again and again, Ling doesn't let fear stop her from telling the stories she thinks the world deserves to hear.

"TRY TO ACCOMPLISH THINGS YOU HAVE ALWAYS DREAMT OF WHILE YOU CAN."
—LISA LING

FEARLESS FACTS

➔ **BORN:** August 30, 1973, Sacramento, California, U.S.A. ➔ **OCCUPATION:** Journalist, television presenter ➔ **BOLDEST MOMENT:** Putting her safety on the line to report the news

WIELDING THE PEN
REMARKABLE WRITERS

What does it take to change the world? Other women in this chapter broke down barriers using fire hoses and fighter jets. But the heroines on these pages wielded a much smaller tool: the pen. Using sharp wits and wise words, they wrote their own names into the history books.

FIRST WOMAN TO WIN THE PULITZER PRIZE:
Edith Wharton (1862–1937)

Edith Wharton attempted to write her first novel when she was just 11 years old. But Edith's parents expected her to become a wealthy New York socialite, and they didn't think writing was very ladylike. It is rumored that when they found a book of poems Edith had secretly printed, they destroyed it.

But Wharton was determined to go her own way, despite her family's disapproval. She used her sharp wit and insider's view to criticize America's upper class. In 1921, she became the first woman to win the prestigious Pulitzer Prize for fiction, for her book *The Age of Innocence*.

MOTHER OF THE MODERN NOVEL:
Jane Austen (1775–1817)

When British novelist Jane Austen was young, there was only one way a woman could make a better life for herself: marry well. Born into poverty, 20-year-old Austen fell in love with a wealthy young man named Thomas Lefroy. She was sure he would propose to her, but while she was waiting for the big moment, he left town.

This heartbreaking experience might have contributed to Austen's deep understanding of the ups and

Emily Dickinson left school when she was a teen-ager and spent the rest of her days in a Victorian house in Amherst, Massachusetts, U.S.A., shut away from the outside world. Though her life was largely one of isolation, she was an avid reader and wrote many letters, scribbling away late into the night at a tiny desk in an upstairs corner bedroom. When Dickinson died in 1886, her family dis-covered what else she had been penning: nearly 1,800 poems in 40 hand-bound volumes.

Today, Dickinson is regarded as one of the greatest poets in American history—male or female. She used unusual structure and punctuation in her poems and was known for her short, moving verse. She was never famous during her lifetime, but her work changed poetry forever. Many modern poets cite Dickinson's unique style as a major influence on their work.

WORD WIZARD:
William Shakespeare (1564–1616)

DARING DUDE

The king is dead, murdered by a wicked brother who takes control of the kingdom. The king's son, the prince, is forced to flee to a neighboring land, where the ghost of his dead father urges his son to retake his rightful place as ruler.

Sound familiar? That's the plot of Disney's *The Lion King*, released in 1994. It's also the plot of *Hamlet*, written by English playwright and poet William Shakespeare around the year 1600. Most literary historians agree that Shakespeare is history's greatest writer of the English language. As he produced one crowd-pleaser after another, he became famous for his characters, tales, wit, and way with words. The Bard changed the English language, coining more than 2,000 newfangled words that are still fashionable today, includ-ing "newfangled" and "fashionable."

downs of romance. She began writing novels, such as *Sense and Sensibility* and *Pride and Prejudice*, about the trials, tribulations, and miscommunications of people falling in love and getting married. Her novels are insightful looks at everyday life. It was unusual at the time, but has since influenced how modern novels are written. Austen's writ-ing was very popular in her time, but, because there were hardly any woman authors in the early 1800s, she wrote anonymously. It was only after her death that the world learned that their beloved novelist had been a woman.

Rolling Up THEIR SLEEVES

WOMEN, WAR, AND WORK

When America entered World War II, in December 1941, men were forced to leave their jobs to become soldiers. Factories everywhere stood empty. Suddenly, there was no one to make badly needed supplies for soldiers on the front lines. So the government launched a campaign to encourage women to join the workforce. This poster—featuring a woman nicknamed Rosie the Riveter, sleeves rolled up and ready to take on the world—is the most famous image from that movement.

Inspired, America's women stepped up to the challenge. They learned to operate machines and make airplanes, bullets, and weapons—a dangerous job because of the risk of accidental explosions. But these brave females faced the risk and filled the jobs left empty by men on the battlefield, carrying their country through one of the most trying times in its history.

We Can Do It!

THE REAL ROSIE

Who was the woman in the famous poster? Historians think she was based on a real person named Geraldine Hoff Doyle. In 1942, when Doyle was 17 years old, she went to work for the American Broach & Machine Co. in Ann Arbor, Michigan, U.S.A. She was operating a metal-stamping machine, her brunette hair covered by a polka-dot bandanna, when a press photographer snapped a photo of her.

Artist J. Howard Miller, who had been commissioned to create posters to inspire factory workers, reportedly saw the photo, and it may have influenced the bandanna-clad woman in his famous drawing. The poster would later go on to be a symbol of the feminist movement. According to her daughter, Stephanie Gregg, Doyle had no idea of her tie to the famous poster until the mid-1980s. "She was tickled to recognize that she was the inspiration for so many women," said Gregg.

WOMEN AT WORK

During the war, more than six million women joined the workforce. They became welders, electricians, engineers, and chemists, and operated streetcars, buses, cranes, and tractors. The aviation industry saw the greatest increase in female workers—from just one percent before the war to 65 percent by 1943.

Some women even joined the armed services. The WACs, or members of the Women's Army Corps, operated switchboards, delivered mail, and worked as mechanics. Most served in the United States, but some went abroad—WACs landed on the beaches of Normandy, France, just a few weeks after the D-Day invasion on June 6, 1944.

Other women became Women Airforce Service Pilots, or WASPs. These women, who were already pilots before war broke out, became the first females to fly American military planes. They delivered new planes from factories to Air Force bases, transported cargo, and helped run training missions. More than 1,000 WASPs served in the war, and 38 of them lost their lives. They weren't officially recognized as part of the military until 1977.

Muriel SIEBERT

THE FIRST LADY OF WALL STREET

In Muriel Siebert's day, the trading floor of the New York Stock Exchange was no place for the faint of heart. People in blue jackets frantically waved pieces of paper, with sweat dripping down their faces, while gesturing with wild hand signals and screaming to be heard over each other. They made and lost fortunes every day in one of the most intense and stressful jobs out there. And, until 1967, women weren't allowed to participate. Siebert changed that.

NEW YORK, NEW YORK

In 1954, with her $500 life savings in her pocket, 26-year-old college dropout Muriel Siebert hopped into a used car and drove from Ohio U.S.A., to New York City to make her fortune. She got a job as a trainee doing research for the brokerage firm Bache and Co. for $65 a week. More senior male co-workers gave her the industries none of them wanted, like aviation, which wasn't seen as a big moneymaker in an age when railroads dominated. Luckily for Siebert, airplanes took off, and she was at the helm of the budding business.

When she found out that men doing the same work were earning more money, Siebert quit to find a new job. She had trouble getting interviews—until she changed the name on her résumé from "Muriel Siebert" to "M. Siebert" to conceal her gender. Siebert never could find a job that would pay her

> "THERE WERE NO FEMALE ROLE MODELS, SO I JUST BLAZED MY OWN PATH."
> —MURIEL SIEBERT

FEARLESS FACTS

→ **BORN:** September 12, 1928, Cleveland, Ohio, U.S.A. → **DIED:** August 24, 2013, New York, New York, U.S.A.
→ **OCCUPATION:** Wall Street analyst → **BOLDEST MOMENT:** Building a business empire in a man's world

equally—so she decided to go into business for herself. To do it, she needed a seat on the New York Stock Exchange, a position no woman had held before. When she applied, in 1967, Wall Street was turned upside down. People were shocked that a woman dared ask for the job. The New York Stock Exchange insisted on a specific condition—that Siebert had to get a bank loan to cover $300,000 of the $445,000 seat price. It took two years for Siebert to persuade a bank to loan her the money, but she finally got the seat on December 28, 1967. It would be a decade before another woman would repeat the feat. "For ten years," Siebert later said, "it was 1,365 men and me."

Muriel Siebert, at her desk in 1977 (above), donated millions of dollars to help other women get started in finance and business.

FEMINIST FIGHTER

Siebert made big strides toward carving out a place for women in the world of finance. But she had to fight for every victory. In the early 1970s, she and her male colleagues attended a meeting at a Manhattan social club called the Union League Club. The club didn't allow female members, and when Siebert arrived for her meeting, they made her go through the kitchen and walk up the back stairs. To show their support, when the meeting was over, her male colleagues joined her by exiting the way she had come.

But the men around Siebert didn't always back her up. For 20 years after she bought her seat on the stock exchange, the only women's bathroom was far away down a flight of stairs. In 1987, Siebert decided she wouldn't stand for that any more. She told the exchange's chairman that if he did not finally install a ladies' room on the floor by the end of the year, she would have a portable toilet delivered. The chairman caved, and Siebert finally got her restroom.

She went on to break barrier after barrier. Siebert became the first woman to own and operate her own firm and the first female state superintendent of banking for the state of New York, and she was—for a brief time—the first self-made female billionaire. In a system intent on holding her back, Siebert became one of the best in the business.

OPTIMISTIC GENIUS: Elon Musk (1971–) DARING DUDE

This business trailblazer flies his own jet, has a race car, and invests megabucks in everything from spaceships to alternative energy resources. Elon Musk is a South African–born whiz kid who struck it rich in Internet start-ups before investing in his real passion: technologies for a better future.

Musk's SpaceX company builds rockets to reach Earth's orbit and beyond. (He plans to eventually colonize Mars!) His Tesla company builds electric cars that go farther and faster on a single charge without burning a drop of gasoline—better than clunkier previous models. He co-founded SolarCity to make sun-fueled energy systems for houses and cities, helping residents rely less on the fossil fuels that contribute to the warming of the planet. It's an ambitious collection of companies for a man who could have retired after making his first billion. Musk is investing in a brighter tomorrow for everyone—or at least finding us another planet to live on if things here don't work out.

RUNNING THE SHOW
TRAILBLAZERS IN BUSINESS

There's an invisible upper limit—called the glass ceiling—that has long kept women from advancing to the top of the business world. But for these heroines, it wasn't a barrier; it was a challenge. On their rise to the top, they shattered the glass ceiling—and became role models for other businesswomen.

BEST YET!
FOR ALL THE FAMILY!

MADAM WALKER'S
ALL-PURPOSE
HAIR CONDITIONING CREAM

"FOR PERFECT DRESSING

HAIR-CARE HEROINE:
Madam C. J. Walker (1867–1919)

At age seven, Madam C. J. Walker was an orphan laboring in the cotton fields. When she grew up, she worked as a washerwoman, supporting her daughter on $1.50 a day. But her life changed when she heard the words of civil rights activist Booker T. Washington, who called for African Americans to bring themselves up in the world by developing skills and working hard.

Walker decided that her future was in hair-care products. Around 1907, she began making her own shampoos and styling products. They were wildly successful, and within a few years, she had made $250,000—about the equivalent of $4 million today! She was one of the first American women—and the first black American woman—to become a self-made millionaire. She was also one of the largest employers of African-American women, with more than 3,000 black factory workers and 20,000 cosmetics salespeople. She generously shared her riches, donating to orphanages, schools, and civil rights organizations.

MAKEUP MOGUL: Mary Kay Ash (1918–2001)

Mary Kay Ash was one of the best salespeople in her company. But for more than a decade, she watched man after man get promoted over her. Ash finally had enough and quit.

At age 45, with just $5,000, she founded cosmetics company Mary Kay, Inc., and used an unusual strategy to guide her business—the golden rule: Treat others as you wish to be treated. She believed that praise was the surest way to make her employees successful, and she celebrated their accomplishments, famously rewarding her top salespeople every year with pink Cadillacs. Today, Mary Kay, Inc. is one of the most successful companies in the world, and Ash's business model has been mirrored time and time again.

BUSINESS WIZARD: Sheryl Sandberg (1969–)

In high school, Sheryl Sandberg was voted Most Likely to Succeed. But she thought that was uncool, so she made her friend on the yearbook staff award it to somebody else. A lifetime of success would prove to Sandberg how silly that was. By age 38, she was Google's vice president of global online sales and operations and, in 2008, was hired as the chief operating officer (COO) of Facebook, where she ran the company's business side. She was the first woman to serve on Facebook's board of directors. In Sandberg's first three years on the job, Facebook multiplied its users and earnings by ten times. Today, she lectures and writes, encouraging women to be ambitious and take on leadership roles. "Leadership is not bullying, and leadership is not aggression," Sandberg has said. "Leadership is the expectation that you can use your voice for good. That you can make the world a better place."

TALK SHOW SUPERSTAR: Oprah Winfrey (1954–)

Oprah Winfrey was born into extreme poverty: Sometimes, because her family couldn't afford clothes, she had to wear potato sacks. Today, she's worth an estimated $3 billion and is the only black woman on *Forbes*'s list of the 400 richest people in America.

Winfrey succeeded through talent and determination. In 1971, she became the first black female news anchor at WTVF in Nashville, Tennessee, U.S.A. In 1983, she started working at *A.M. Chicago*, the lowest-rated talk show in Chicago—and within a month turned it into the highest-rated one. Three years later, its name was changed to *The Oprah Winfrey Show*. Winfrey's warm-hearted personality earned her loyal fans, and the show aired for 25 seasons, from 1986 to 2011, making it one of the longest-running daytime television shows in history. Winfrey has raised millions for charitable organizations. Among many other causes, she's donated to victims of Hurricane Katrina and to girls' education in South Africa.

BENEVOLENT BILLIONAIRE: Bill Gates (1955–)

DARING DUDE

This computer whiz co-founded Microsoft and in 1985 pioneered the Windows operating system, which was easier to use than the clunky interfaces of the day. His software transformed computers from business machines into essential desktop devices for work and fun. Gates eventually accomplished his mission of putting a personal computer in nearly every home in America. In the process, he became one of the richest men in the world—and then started giving his money away. With his wife, he donated $30 billion to form the Bill & Melinda Gates Foundation, which works to improve education, water quality, and sanitation across the world. One of the foundation's projects is a machine that turns human waste into drinking water.

Carol BURNETT

FIRST LADY OF LAUGHS

Carol Burnett is widely considered one of the funniest people ever to grace the small screen. But her life didn't start out so charmed. Carol's parents divorced when she was very young, and the eight-year-old Carol went to live with her grandmother. Carol and her grandmother didn't have much: They shared a pull-down bed in a one-room apartment in Los Angeles, California, U.S.A. But they did have a passion for the movies, going as often as eight times a week.

Burnett enrolled at the University of California, Los Angeles, where she was required to take an acting class to get her degree. Burnett was terrified to get up on stage, but when she performed a comedy scene, something amazing happened—people thought she was funny! She later remembered thinking, "This is it. I want to, the rest of my life, make people laugh." And she did.

Burnett moved to New York in 1954 and worked in musicals and cabaret shows and eventually on television. She was an enormous hit; audiences loved her quirky facial expressions and talent for physical comedy. But when she asked for her own variety show, her bosses at CBS were shocked. Back then, variety shows—the most popular shows on TV—were all hosted by men. But Burnett was determined and, in 1967, launched *The Carol Burnett Show*. It ran for 11 seasons and won 25 awards. Today, it's considered a comedy classic. Burnett is a pioneer who paved the way for women to become comedians—and made the world laugh while doing it.

> "WHEN YOU HAVE A DREAM, YOU'VE GOT TO GRAB IT AND NEVER LET GO."
> —CAROL BURNETT

FEARLESS FACTS

➔ **BORN:** April 26, 1933, San Antonio, Texas, U.S.A. ➔ **OCCUPATION:** Actress, comedian, writer
➔ **BOLDEST MOMENT:** Becoming the first woman to host a television variety show

Tina FEY

When Tiny Fey was growing up, she wasn't allowed to stay up until 11:30 p.m., when the comedy sketch show *Saturday Night Live* came on television. So her older brother would act out the skits for her the next day. Little Tina had no idea that someday she would be one of the show's stars.

In middle school, Tina made up her mind to become the class clown. When she cracked jokes and her classmates laughed in response, she knew she'd found what she wanted to do for the rest of her life. After college, Fey took off for Chicago, Illinois, U.S.A., to join Second City, a famous acting and comedy school. After two years of classes, Fey was invited to go on tour with Second City. The pace was exhausting—she performed eight shows a week for two years—but her drive to succeed kept her going.

In 1997, Fey made a bold move. She sent a script to *Saturday Night Live* and asked the producers to consider her for a position on the writing staff. They loved her sharp wit, and Fey got the job. Just two years later, she was promoted to head writer—the first time a woman had held the position in the show's 27-year history. She wrote sketches that featured women, giving female comics more screen time than they'd had in the past. In 2000, she appeared on the show herself, becoming the first woman since 1982 to host the news comedy segment *Weekend Update.* Fey went on to write the hit movie *Mean Girls* and create the award-winning TV show *30 Rock.* In 2010, she was awarded the Mark Twain Prize for American Humor—the youngest person ever to receive the honor.

"THE DIFFERENCE BETWEEN MALE COMEDY WRITERS AND FEMALE COMEDY WRITERS IS THAT THE MALE ONES ARE TALLER AND WEIGH MORE."
—TINA FEY

FEARLESS FACTS

➔ **BORN:** May 18, 1970, Upper Darby, Pennsylvania, U.S.A. ➔ **OCCUPATION:** Actress, comedian, writer, producer ➔ **BOLDEST MOMENT:** Changing the face of *Saturday Night Live*

MOMENT OF BRAVERY

When disaster came, how did this quick-thinking teacher offer a lesson in courage?

THE SITUATION

On May 20, 2013, in Moore, Oklahoma, U.S.A., 44-year-old Rhonda Crosswhite was teaching her sixth-grade glass at Plaza Towers Elementary School. There had been severe weather the previous few days, and the citizens of Moore were on high alert. Oklahoma is part of an area of the United States nicknamed Tornado Alley for the twisters that commonly strike there. But nobody anticipated how bad this storm would be. Around 3 p.m., the sky darkened. A little wisp of a cloud suddenly transformed into a giant spinning funnel—and headed straight toward Moore.

The school's tornado sirens rang out, and Crosswhite reacted quickly. She herded her students out of the classroom and into a bathroom in the building's interior, where they would be more protected. But then she heard a noise like a giant train. The monstrous one-mile (1.6-km)-wide twister was slamming directly into the school! As Crosswhite and the kids stood there, the tornado began to tear the building apart.

Crosswhite wanted to protect her students, no matter the cost. With the tornado screaming over her head, Crosswhite kept her cool. She ran into a stall with six students, told them to get on the floor, and lay on top of them, using her body as a shield to protect the kids from flying debris. The 200-mile-an-hour (322-km/h) winds embedded glass shards into her skin and sent a cinder block flying into her back. But Crosswhite didn't move. Even though she was terrified, she stayed strong for her students, telling them, "We're going to be fine, guys. Stay calm." When the storm finally stopped, Crosswhite and her students climbed out of the debris—and saw that the school had been turned into a pile of rubble.

THE LEGACY

The tornado caused massive destruction in Moore. When the tornado passed and the survivors emerged, they saw trees snapped in half, roofs of houses sheared off, and fences ripped out and carried away. It was the most deadly tornado to strike the United States that year. More than a thousand homes were destroyed, and 24 people were killed. All the students Crosswhite protected walked away from the disaster. When she was called a hero for her bravery, Crosswhite rejected the praise, saying, "Every morning at nine, those children become my children. I was just taking care of my kids."

Legendary
LADIES

Throughout history, tales of brave women and their heroic deeds have been the source of inspiration for countless fearless females. Storytellers have passed these tales—some tall, some true—from generation to generation, each time encouraging a new era of women to go out and do great things. This chapter celebrates women who battled bravely for what is right, whether in real life or just in legend, and inspired others to do the same.

Statute of Diana the Huntress, also known
as Artemis, in County Wicklow, Ireland

Athena

WISE WARRIOR

According to Greek mythology, Zeus, the king of the Greek gods, one day came down with a terrible headache. It throbbed and ached, growing worse as the day went on. Finally, the pain became unbearable. Desperate for relief, Zeus asked the blacksmith god Hephaestus for help. Hephaestus picked up a heavy ax, swung his mighty arms—and split Zeus's forehead open. From the crack sprung Zeus's daughter, the goddess Athena, fully grown and ready for battle.

GODDESS OF WISDOM

Even though Athena started out as a headache, Zeus grew to love her the best of all his children; he even let her use his weapons, such as his mighty thunderbolt. And because she was the goddess of wisdom, Athena was his prime adviser. She used her impressive brain to bring humans valuable gifts, such as the plow, the rake, the chariot, and the art of navigation. Athena's wisdom was tested when both she and the ocean god, Poseidon, wanted to be the patron of a new city. The two deities had almost come to blows when Athena devised a compromise: Whoever gave the new city the best gift would win the honor. Poseidon agreed, and a huge crowd gathered to watch the two gods face off.

Poseidon went first. He raised his trident and slammed it into the ground. From the place he struck, a spring of water began to flow. The people *oohed* and *ahhed*—but when they tasted the water, they found it to be as salty as the sea Poseidon came from. Then came Athena's turn. The

IN GREEK MYTHOLOGY, ATHENA IS THE GODDESS OF WISDOM AND WAR.

FEARLESS FACTS

→ **BORN:** Mount Olympus, Greece → **OCCUPATION:** Goddess → **BOLDEST MOMENT:** Using smarts as her strength

goddess didn't use flashy gestures. Instead, she simply knelt and planted something in the ground: an olive tree. The fruit of the olive tree fed the people, and its branches became fuel and wood for building. Though Athena's gift was simple, it was superior, and she won the honor of becoming the city's patron goddess. Athens is still named for her today.

GODDESS OF WAR

Athena and her brother, Ares, were both deities of war. But unlike Ares, who fought with violence, Athena's weapons of choice were strategy and logic. Her methods were so effective that Athena never lost a fight. The goddess of victory, Nike, always followed her into battle.

During the Trojan War—which historians now think was a real war that may have occurred around 1180 B.C.—Athena advised the Greek hero Odysseus, helping him devise a clever way to get inside the walled city of Troy. One morning, the Trojans woke up to see their enemies, the Greeks, sailing off into the sunset. In their place was a giant wooden horse outside the city gates. Thinking it was a gift, the Trojans took the horse inside the city and spent the night feasting and celebrating their victory over the Greeks. But that night, after all the Trojans had fallen asleep, Greek soldiers emerged from their hiding place inside the horse. They opened the city gates and let in the returning Greek army, which conquered Troy and won the war.

The Greeks revered Athena for her wisdom and compassion, and she was one of their most beloved gods. Athena is a reminder that intelligence and logic can be the most powerful weapons in any battle.

The Parthenon (above left); depiction of Athena emerging from the head of Zeus (above right)

QUICK-WITTED KING: Odysseus
DARING DUDE

Odysseus' victory over the Trojans is but one chapter in a legend that has the hero—star of the ancient Greek poem *The Odyssey*—outsmarting a who's who of mythological monsters. The hero bested the Cyclops by clinging to the belly of a ram to sneak out of his cave. Then, he outwitted the Sirens, beautiful but deadly creatures whose enchanting songs lured sailors to shipwreck on the rocky coast of their island. Astute Odysseus plugged his crew's ears with wax and ordered himself tied to the ship's mast so he could enjoy their music, minus the deadly consequences. Odysseus may have been brave and strong, but it was the hero's cleverness that ultimately got him through his epic adventures.

DEITIES AND DAMES
GRECIAN GIRLS WORTH WORSHIPPING

The ancient Greeks didn't have television, video games, or comic books. So instead they entertained themselves with stories, kind of like you're doing right now. They told tales about people with incredible powers who battled monsters for the fate of the world.

FLEET FEET: Atalanta the Fierce

The mythical heroine Atalanta was abandoned as a baby by her parents (who had been hoping for a boy) and raised in the forest by a bear. She grew up to be just as ferocious as her adoptive mother. She became one of the best hunters in Greece and also one of the fastest mortals. When she joined a group of heroes on a hunt for a boar that was terrorizing the countryside, many of the men were angry to have a woman in their ranks. But Atalanta proved her worth when she became the first to hit the beast. Atalanta had no use for men. When her father—with whom she had reunited—tried to marry her off, she said she would marry any man who could beat her in a footrace. Man after man tried to win her hand, but none were fast enough to defeat her.

INDEPENDENT GODDESS: Artemis the Huntress

Artemis was another Greek woman who loved the independent life. But, unlike Atalanta, Artemis was a goddess who could use her divine powers to keep suitors at bay. As the goddess of the hunt, she was worshipped by hunters, who prayed to her to grant them strength and health. But they had to be careful to stay on her good side. One day, a hunter named Actaeon was out hunting with his pack of hounds when he wandered deep into the forest and happened upon the goddess bathing in a pool. Furious that a mere mortal man dared to watch her bathe, Artemis used magic to send water flying at Actaeon. When the drops hit him, they transformed him into a deer.

SUPERMOM: Determined Demeter

Young Persephone was having a lovely time frolicking in a field of flowers when her world came crashing down—literally. The Earth split open, and Hades, the king of the underworld, snatched her up and carried her off to his subterranean palace. Persephone's mother, Demeter, frantically searched for her daughter and grieved terribly when Persephone could not be found. Demeter was the goddess of the harvest, and, in the wake of her grief, fields became barren, and both animals and people starved. But angry Demeter would allow nothing to grow until her daughter was returned to her. So Zeus, king of the gods, ordered Persephone returned. But because Persephone had tasted the food of the underworld, she would have to descend back to Hades for part of every year. According to Greek mythology, the meadows flower and the grain sprouts each spring when Demeter joyfully welcomes her daughter, and the plants die every winter when she must again grieve her daughter's departure.

TRIPLE THREAT: The Fates

More powerful than any of the gods were the three sisters called the Fates. Greeks feared and respected the Fates because these sisters were in charge of when life began and ended and what happened in the middle. Three days after a child was born, the fabled sisters would come calling to determine its destiny. Clotho was the spinner, who spun the thread of life. Lachesis measured the thread, determining what the baby's life would hold. And Atropos, the smallest of the three sisters, was the most powerful: She cut the thread, deciding when life would end.

MAN OF MUSCLE: Hercules

Brawny Hercules was the son of a mortal woman and Zeus, the king of the gods. Zeus's goddess wife, Hera, wasn't happy with the situation, and wasted no time taking it out on her husband's beloved half-god son. She sent poisonous snakes into Hercules' crib, but the muscle-bound baby crushed them before you could say "goo-goo, ga-gaaahhh!" Hera's harassment of Hercules continued throughout his life. She dreamed up 12 deadly labors for Hercules, such as conquering the three-headed hound Cerberus and a nine-headed serpent called the Hydra. Just like a modern superhero, Hercules always survived for the sequel.

Gaia

MOTHER OF THE EARTH

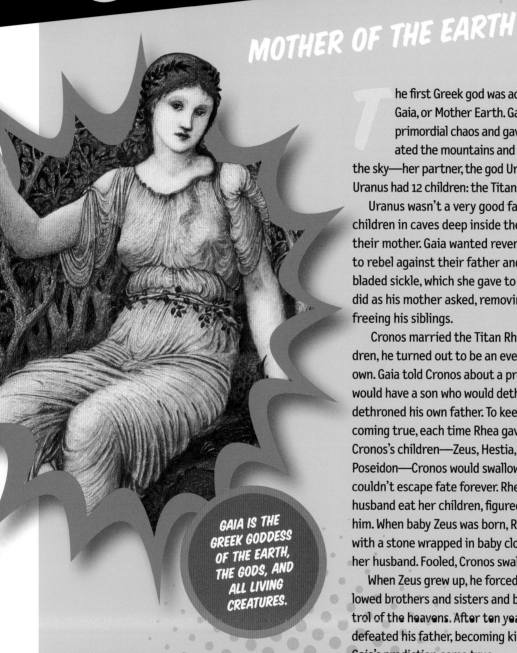

GAIA IS THE GREEK GODDESS OF THE EARTH, THE GODS, AND ALL LIVING CREATURES.

The first Greek god was actually a goddess, named Gaia, or Mother Earth. Gaia created herself out of primordial chaos and gave birth to all life. She created the mountains and the sea. She also created the sky—her partner, the god Uranus. Together, Gaia and Uranus had 12 children: the Titans.

Uranus wasn't a very good father. He imprisoned his children in caves deep inside the Earth—the body of their mother. Gaia wanted revenge. She asked the Titans to rebel against their father and shaped a great flint-bladed sickle, which she gave to her son Cronos. Cronos did as his mother asked, removing Uranus from power and freeing his siblings.

Cronos married the Titan Rhea, and when she bore children, he turned out to be an even worse father than his own. Gaia told Cronos about a prophecy—that one day, he would have a son who would dethrone him, just like he had dethroned his own father. To keep the prediction from coming true, each time Rhea gave birth to one of her and Cronos's children—Zeus, Hestia, Demeter, Hera, Hades, and Poseidon—Cronos would swallow the baby. But Cronos couldn't escape fate forever. Rhea, tired of watching her husband eat her children, figured out a way to outsmart him. When baby Zeus was born, Rhea swapped the infant with a stone wrapped in baby clothes and presented it to her husband. Fooled, Cronos swallowed the stone.

When Zeus grew up, he forced Cronos to expel his swallowed brothers and sisters and battled the Titans for control of the heavens. After ten years of waging war, he finally defeated his father, becoming king of the gods and making Gaia's prediction come true.

FEARLESS FACTS

➲ **BORN:** At the beginning of all things ➲ **OCCUPATION:** Goddess ➲ **BOLDEST MOMENT:** Creating herself, the mountains, the sea, and the sky

The Queen OF SHEBA

MOTHER OF A NATION

Even though no one knows what the Queen of Sheba's name actually was, she is one of the world's most important religious figures. She appears in texts that are sacred to Jews, Muslims, and Christians and is believed by Ethiopians to have been the mother of their first emperor.

According to legend, the Queen of Sheba had heard that Israel's King Solomon was a ruler with great wisdom. She wanted to see for herself whether he deserved his reputation. She traveled to his palace, carrying magnificent treasures from her land: camels loaded with spices, jewels, and gold.

Solomon was also curious about his visitor. He had heard that her left foot was like a goat's. Legend says that Solomon used the shiny palace floor to discover the truth. When the queen arrived, Solomon saw the reflection of her foot in the floor. But then the queen's goatlike hoof turned back into a normal foot.

Behind the myths and legends, there was a real Queen of Sheba. Little is certain about her life, but most scholars think she was born late in the 11th century B.C. and ruled an area in northern Africa that is today Ethiopia. In 2012, an archaeologist named Louise Schofield was exploring there when she found a stone slab marked with a sun and moon—the signature of the land of Sheba. Schofield crawled under it and found an inscription in Sabaean, the ancient language the queen would have spoken. Schofield excavated and uncovered an ancient goldmine—possibly the source of the treasure that the queen carried to Solomon.

HISTORIANS NOW THINK SHE WAS A REAL PERSON WHO RULED AN AREA IN NORTHERN AFRICA THAT IS TODAY ETHIOPIA.

FEARLESS FACTS

➔ **BORN:** Possibly late in the 11th century B.C. ➔ **OCCUPATION:** Queen, religious figure
➔ **BOLDEST MOMENT:** Bringing a new faith back to her homeland

WOMEN OF ACTION
COURAGEOUS CHARACTERS OF TV AND FILM

Step aside, James Bond. These action heroines may not wear tuxedos, but they're every bit as bold, brave, and cool under pressure. Whether facing down aliens from another planet or demons from another world, these stars of TV and film used their smarts and skill to beat the baddies.

PROTECTING THE INNOCENT:
Xena, Warrior Princess

When Xena was a child, she watched in horror as an evil warlord destroyed her village and killed her brother. Xena formed an army to protect her fellow peasants. But then, after becoming obsessed with power, she transformed into a ruthless conqueror herself. Her relationship with the good hero Hercules changed her, however, and Xena swore to devote her life to protecting the innocent.

Through the six seasons of the television show *Xena, Warrior Princess*, Xena travels the world—and even journeys to the underworld—on her mission. This leather-clad woman warrior used her formidable fighting skills to conquer evildoers and, at the same time, battled internal demons from her past.

REBEL, REBEL: Princess Leia

Luke Skywalker gets all the credit as the star of the original *Star Wars* movie trilogy. But his twin sister, Princess Leia, was every bit as much of a hero. When Leia was born to Anakin Skywalker, a Jedi knight who would later turn to the dark side and become the villainous Darth Vader, she was sent to grow up in safety on the planet Alderaan. There, she became a politician: the youngest senator ever elected to the Imperial Senate. She secretly used her position to help the Rebel Army fight the dark side.

On one mission, Leia's Rebel ship acquired the plans for the Death Star, a superweapon capable of destroying an entire planet. When her ship was

TAKING A BITE OUT OF CRIME:
Buffy the Vampire Slayer

In the late 1980s, writer Joss Whedon had an unusual idea for a horror movie. He was tired of scripts that featured blond female victims getting killed off. What if he flipped the stereotype on its head and made the blonde a bold heroine? The result: Buffy Summers, an ordinary high school girl who had an ordinary life ... until one day when she was approached by a mysterious man who revealed that Buffy was actually fated to be a vampire slayer. Unbeknownst to her, in a turn of unfortunate geography, her high school was located above a portal to the demon world. Vampires and other supernatural beings filtered through her town, and all of a sudden it was Buffy's job to protect her friends and family. After a brutal attack on fellow students, Buffy knew she had to act. With the help of her friends, Buffy used strength, skill, and smarts to take down one beastly being after another.

RAD LIEUTENANT:
Ellen Ripley

In the 1979 movie *Alien*, the year was 2122 and Lieutenant Ellen Ripley was deep in hypersleep aboard the spaceship USCSS *Nostromo*. Little did she know her mission was about to turn into a nightmare. While investigating an abandoned spacecraft, the *Nostromo*'s crew accidentally brought an alien parasite back aboard with them. The creature began terrorizing the ship, growing bigger and preying on the crew. Her companions disappeared one by one, until Ripley was the only one left. As the monster stalked her through the empty ship, Ripley kept a cool head. Using logic and considerable bravery, she stopped the alien once and for all ... at least until *Aliens*, the sequel.

intercepted by Darth Vader's army, the plucky princess thought fast. She managed to hide the plans inside the robot R2-D2 before she was taken prisoner. Because of Leia's bravery and quick mind, the first Death Star was eventually destroyed.

In later adventures, Princess Leia continued to fight for the Rebels and against the Empire and the dark side of the Force. She posed as a bounty hunter to free Han Solo from his unfortunate encasement in carbonite, put an end to the villainous Jabba the Hut, made friends with Ewoks, and eventually helped destroy the shield generator protecting the second Death Star.

Wonder WOMAN

BRAINY, BRAWNY, AND BOLD

EARRINGS

Wonder Woman's earrings aren't just for looks. They allow her to breathe in oxygen-free environments like outer space.

TIARA

Wonder Woman uses her tiara like a boomerang. With the super-human strength she has thanks to her Amazonian blood, Wonder Woman can hurl the tiara with enough force to cut through almost anything.

MAGIC BRACELETS

All the Amazon women from Paradise Island wear special bracelets, symbolizing the time when, long ago, the Amazons (see page 82) were enslaved to the mythical Greek hero Hercules. The bracelets are bulletproof and, if crossed, form a shield, giving Wonder Woman a powerful defense. But they're also her greatest weakness: If Wonder Woman loses her bracelets, she goes crazy with rage. And if a villain fuses them together, she grows weak.

GOLDEN LASSO OF TRUTH

When Wonder Woman needed a weapon worthy of a superhero, she went to the Greek blacksmith god Hephaestus. From the belt of the goddess Aphrodite, he forged her a lasso. Wonder Woman's magical lasso is unbreakable and infinitely stretchable. When Wonder Woman uses it to truss up a villain, he has no choice but to tell her the truth.

INVISIBLE PLANE

Wonder Woman can fly, of course. But when she needs to get somewhere fast, she hops into her invisible plane. The plane represents Pegasus, the mythical flying horse. As real-world technology grew along with the Wonder Woman comics, the invisible plane became an invisible jet.

Wonder Woman is the most famous superheroine of all time. Aside from Batman and Superman, no other comic book character has been around as long as this legendary lady. Since she first appeared in comic books in 1941, she's been made into countless action figures and has adorned T-shirts, lunch boxes, and magazine covers snapped up by generations of girls and boys.

Wonder Woman was created by William Marston, a psychologist whose research on the detection of deception led to the development of the lie detector test. Marston believed the attitude that women were inferior to men was wrong, and he wanted to use his new comic book heroine to change that. He made Wonder Woman the only female member of the superhero group called the Justice Society. When another writer penned a 1942 comic that showed the male superheroes heading off to war while leaving Wonder Woman behind to answer the mail, Marston was furious. It was the last time his superheroine was ever left out of the action. Marston showed Wonder Woman encouraging other female characters to be strong, make their own way, and fight for what they wanted. And the public loved her. Wonder Woman gained such a large following that she became the star of her own TV show.

Wonder Woman conquers criminals but, unlike Superman or Batman, doesn't just bring them to justice and move on to the next baddie. She reforms them into upstanding citizens. That might just make her the greatest super-hero of all.

79

Mulan

FEARLESS FIGHTER

Disney's 1998 animated movie *Mulan* tells the story of a girl who goes to war so her aging father doesn't have to. But this heroic tale is more than just a story: Mulan may have been a real person.

GUTSY GIRL

The original story of the legendary heroine comes from an ancient Chinese poem called *The Ballad of Mulan*. Later, the poem was made into many books and operas and became a Chinese folk legend.

In one version of the story, 18-year-old Hua Mulan was passing a beautiful morning washing clothes and practicing martial arts when, suddenly, the town's gong rang. Mulan's heart sank; the sound meant the emperor was recruiting new soldiers for his army.

In most Chinese families, the sons answered the call and joined the fight. But Mulan had no brothers, so the job fell to Mulan's elderly and ailing father. When Mulan saw him getting ready to go to war, she knew that he'd never survive the hardships of battle. So she did the only thing she could think of: She disguised herself as a man so that she could go in his place. Clutching an ancient sword passed down through her family for generations, she headed off to fight.

Unlike the Disney version of the heroine, legend says that the real-life Mulan didn't need a lot of training to prepare her for battle. When Mulan was growing up, her father had thought that girls should know how to fight as well as men, so he had trained Mulan in the art of battle. When she joined the army, she already knew how to wield a sword and use a bow and arrow, and she was excellent at the hand-to-hand combat of martial arts.

> DISGUISED AS A MAN, MULAN JOINED THE EMPEROR'S ARMY SO HER AILING FATHER WOULD NOT HAVE TO FIGHT.

FEARLESS FACTS

➔ **BORN:** ca A.D. 500, China ➔ **DIED:** unknown, China ➔ **OCCUPATION:** Warrior ➔ **BOLDEST MOMENT:** Disguising herself as a man to fight in her father's place

Mulan's fighting skills won her the respect of her fellow soldiers. As she went head-to-head with the fearsome Huns, she proved her bravery in battle. Legend says that Mulan fought for 12 years, and, each year she fought, she was honored by the army with a higher rank.

After the war ended, the emperor offered Mulan the greatest honor of all: a place in his cabinet of advisers. But Mulan said no—all she wanted was a camel that she could ride home to her family. When she finally got home, Mulan changed back into her women's clothes. Her fellow soldiers were shocked to learn that the brave warrior they had fought alongside for more than a decade was female.

A scene from the Disney movie *Mulan* (above left); a depiction of Hua Mulan hand-painted on silk, around the late 19th century (above right)

LASTING LEGEND

For centuries, Mulan's male disguise had been no more than an entertaining detail meant to amuse audiences. But in the 20th century, people started seeing Mulan as a revolutionary who changed society's ideas of what girls are capable of.

We may never know for sure whether Mulan was a real person. But tall tale or true, her story has inspired generations and has continued to be retold for 1,500 years. Over time, the name Hua Mulan has come to mean "heroine" in Chinese society.

MAN VS. MACHINE: John Henry (ca 1840s–1870s)

DARING DUDE

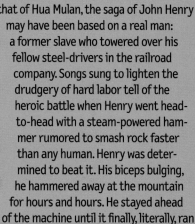

When American folk hero John Henry went to work, the earth trembled and mountains gave way. As a steel-driver, it was his job to hammer metal rods into rock, smashing holes for explosives that blasted holes for train tunnels. Like that of Hua Mulan, the saga of John Henry may have been based on a real man: a former slave who towered over his fellow steel-drivers in the railroad company. Songs sung to lighten the drudgery of hard labor tell of the heroic battle when Henry went head-to-head with a steam-powered hammer rumored to smash rock faster than any human. Henry was determined to beat it. His biceps bulging, he hammered away at the mountain for hours and hours. He stayed ahead of the machine until it finally, literally, ran out of steam.

ON THE WARPATH
FEARSOME FEMALES

The stereotypical soldier may be male, but that doesn't mean women never go to war. Some of the females on these pages are the stuff of legends; others are real-life ladies. All were women not to be messed with. They bravely marched onto the battlefield—and into the history books.

FIGHTER QUEENS: The Amazons

In Greek mythology, the Amazons were a race of wild women warriors. Every Greek hero, from Hercules to Achilles, had to prove his prowess in battle by fighting one of the fearsome queens. There are countless legends about the Amazons' untamed ways; some said they covered their bodies with tattoos, rode horses, and fought ruthlessly on the battlefield. The Amazons were long thought to be only the stuff of legend. But archaeologists recently found the bodies of buried warriors in the graves of an ancient people called the Scythians. The skeletons were laid to rest with their horses and weapons, and their bones showed battle injuries. At first, archaeologists assumed these fighters were all men, but DNA testing revealed that one-third of the Scythian fighters had been female. Some think these were the real Amazons.

CLAWED BUTTERFLY: Itzpapalotl

In Aztec legend, Itzpapalotl was a warrior goddess who ruled over a paradise world called Tamoanchan. This mythical place was the heaven where the gods created the human race and a haven where infants who died would go to spend eternity. Along with other Aztec female deities, Itzpapalotl was also worshipped as a protector of women during childbirth. Sometimes Itzpapalotl would appear as a deer, but most often she would assume her darker form. In that form, she was a skeletal figure with jaguar claws for fingers, eagle claws for toes, and butterfly wings tipped with stone knives.

SAVIOR OF THE CITY:
Agustina de Aragón (1786–1857)

When Napoleon's army invaded the Spanish town of Saragossa in 1808, the townspeople knew they were in trouble. Napoleon and his troops were such fierce fighters that neighboring towns were giving up without protest. But not Saragossa. The citizens gathered their meager weapons, closed Saragossa's 12 gates, and mounted a heroic defense. When 18-year-old Agustina de Aragón—who was carrying food and water to the defenders—saw that French forces were about to breach one of the gates, she took matters into her own hands. She lit the fuse on an unmanned cannon and drove back the enemy, inspiring those around her to keep fighting. Saragossa could only hold out for three months, but its resistance weakened the French. And though her city was defeated, de Aragón wasn't about to give up. She escaped from the besieged city and joined British troops— as the only female officer in that army.

BRAVE SISTER:
Buffalo Calf Road Woman (ca 1850s–1879)

This real-life female fighter was a member of the Cheyenne, a Native American tribe. When the pioneers marched onto Cheyenne territory around 1876, Buffalo Calf Road Woman joined the fight to protect her land. The male warriors weren't too happy about a woman in their ranks, but they changed their tune when Buffalo Calf Road Woman's brother became trapped and surrounded by enemy soldiers. Without hesitation, Buffalo Calf Road Woman charged in and pulled her brother onto her horse and rode to safety. Because of her bravery, Cheyenne warriors named the battle after her, calling it the Battle Where the Girl Saved Her Brother.

WOMAN OF SPORT: Khutulun
(ca 1260–ca 1306)

Khutulun, born around 1260, was a princess of a tribe of nomadic warriors called the Mongols. Though she was royal, Khutulun shunned a life of comfort and civilization, instead devoting her time to the (traditionally male) Mongol arts of horsemanship, archery, and wrestling. When it came time for the princess to marry, she insisted that any potential suitor would have to face her in a wrestling match. If he won, she'd marry him. If he lost, he had to give Khutulun his horses. In no time, Khutulun had won 1,000 horses.

Annie OAKLEY

AMERICA'S FIRST FEMALE SUPERSTAR

Annie Oakley stepped up, toting her .22 rifle. Thirty paces away was her target: a dime her husband gripped between his thumb and forefinger. As the audience held its breath, Annie carefully aimed her weapon, fired, and shot the dime out right of his hand.

Nearly impossible shooting feats like the dime trick were no problem for Annie. She was one of the greatest female sharpshooters in American history. Annie was born Phoebe Ann Oakley Moses in rural Darke County, Ohio, U.S.A. She had a tough childhood. Her father died when she was young, leaving Annie's mother with six children and barely any money to feed them. To help the family survive, Annie was sent to work for people who treated her cruelly. They once left her barefoot out in the snow as punishment for falling asleep before she finished her chores. Though she was only ten years old, Annie was brave enough to run back home. There, she started supporting her family on her own terms: by shooting game and selling it. Annie was so good with a gun that she paid off the mortgage on her mother's house.

When she was 15, Annie entered a shooting contest that pitted her against famous professional sharpshooter Frank Butler. Frank shot 24 out of 25 targets. Annie hit all 25—a perfect round. Frank was astonished that a girl had beaten him. He was also smitten; he and Annie later married. By 1885, Oakley's shooting skill had made her famous. She joined Buffalo Bill's Wild West show and quickly became the star. Oakley was not only a great entertainer but also a savvy businesswoman, earning more than almost any other show member. But she gave most of her earnings away, continuing to support her family and also donating to orphan charities.

> "I AIN'T AFRAID TO LOVE A MAN. I AIN'T AFRAID TO SHOOT HIM, EITHER."
> —ANNIE OAKLEY

FEARLESS FACTS

➲ **BORN:** August 13, 1860, Darke County, Ohio, U.S.A. ➲ **DIED:** November 3, 1926, Greenville, Ohio, U.S.A.
➲ **OCCUPATION:** Markswoman, entertainer ➲ **BOLDEST MOMENT:** Becoming the best shot and using her success to help others

Calamity JANE

Fearless rider. Sharp-eyed shooter. As tough as the cowboys she rode with. In the story of the woman known as Calamity Jane, truth blends with legend.

Calamity Jane was born in Princeton, Missouri, U.S.A., as Martha Cannary. Young Martha loved horseback riding and spending time in the outdoors. When her family embarked on a five-month journey in a wagon train to move from Missouri to Montana, Martha spent most of the trip outside, hunting with the men.

By the time Martha was 12, her parents had died and she had to fend for herself and her five siblings. She took whatever jobs she could get, working as a cook, a nurse, a waitress, and an ox-team driver. At age 18, she served the Army as a scout. To look the part, she dressed like a soldier—and would continue to dress as a man for the rest of her life.

Martha's heroic deeds during this time made her a legend—though she may have embellished some of the tales or made them up entirely. One story says that when her captain was shot and fell off his horse during an ambush, Martha swooped in to scoop him up onto her saddle and save his life. Later he allegedly told her, "I name you Calamity Jane, the heroine of the plains." Jane became a Pony Express rider, carrying mail over one of the route's most dangerous trails, where riders were often held up, their mail and money stolen. But this tough gal had a soft side, once bravely rescuing a runaway stagecoach to save the helpless passengers inside and another time nursing patients during a smallpox epidemic.

"I FIGURE IF A GIRL WANTS TO BE A LEGEND, SHE SHOULD GO AHEAD AND BE ONE."
—CALAMITY JANE

FEARLESS FACTS

➲ **BORN:** ca May 1, 1852, Princeton, Missouri, U.S.A. ➲ **DIED:** August 1, 1903, Terry, South Dakota, U.S.A.
➲ **OCCUPATION:** Army scout, Pony Express rider ➲ **BOLDEST MOMENT:** Defying expectations and facing danger

MOMENT OF BRAVERY

How did this courageous character turn a sad story into a lesson for the ages?

THE SITUATION

Around 442 B.C., ancient Greek playwright Sophocles penned a drama so gut-wrenching that it lives on to modern times. He told the story of Antigone, a Greek girl with a tragic fate. Antigone's two brothers, Eteocles and Polynices, were next in line for the throne of Thebes. When the king died, the brothers agreed to rule jointly, alternating years as king. But after Eteocles' first year was up, the power had gone to his head. He refused to step down.

As Antigone stood by, helpless to stop them, her brothers began a civil war over the throne. Their fight ended with both dead on the battlefield. In their place, Antigone's evil uncle Creon inherited the throne. He declared that Eteocles was to be buried with honor—but Polynices would be left on the battlefield and denied a proper burial. In ancient Greek culture, this was a terrible and shameful punishment. Antigone was horrified.

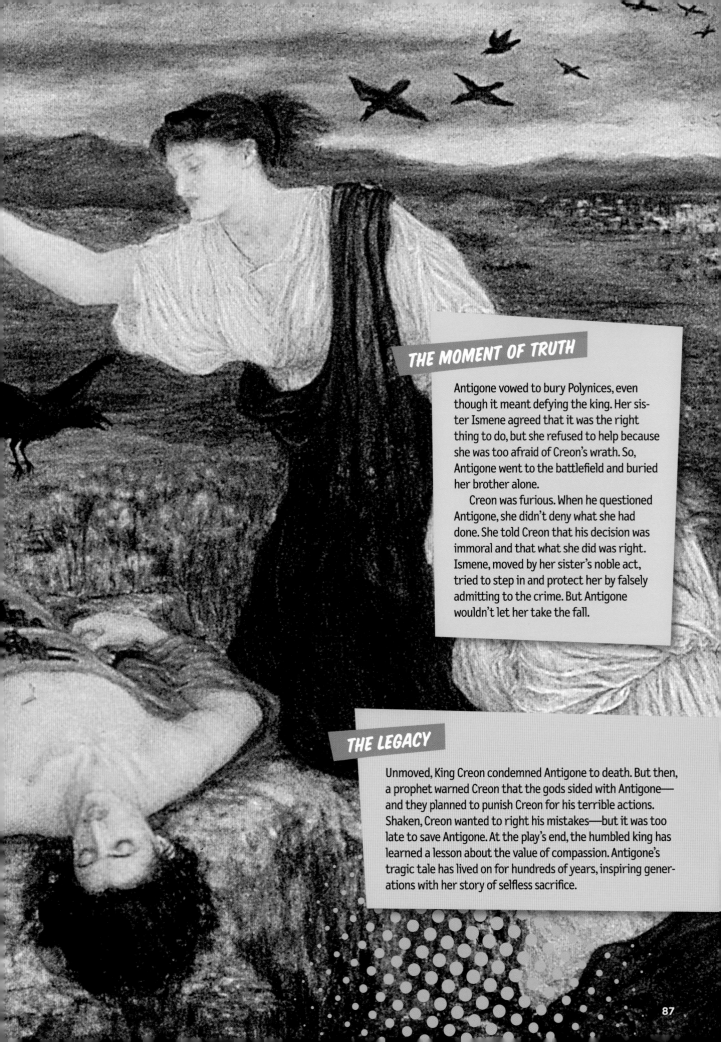

THE MOMENT OF TRUTH

Antigone vowed to bury Polynices, even though it meant defying the king. Her sister Ismene agreed that it was the right thing to do, but she refused to help because she was too afraid of Creon's wrath. So, Antigone went to the battlefield and buried her brother alone.

Creon was furious. When he questioned Antigone, she didn't deny what she had done. She told Creon that his decision was immoral and that what she did was right. Ismene, moved by her sister's noble act, tried to step in and protect her by falsely admitting to the crime. But Antigone wouldn't let her take the fall.

THE LEGACY

Unmoved, King Creon condemned Antigone to death. But then, a prophet warned Creon that the gods sided with Antigone—and they planned to punish Creon for his terrible actions. Shaken, Creon wanted to right his mistakes—but it was too late to save Antigone. At the play's end, the humbled king has learned a lesson about the value of compassion. Antigone's tragic tale has lived on for hundreds of years, inspiring generations with her story of selfless sacrifice.

Daring
DAMES

Think of a brave warrior, marching into the unknown and facing possible peril at every turn. Who do you imagine? Is it a woman parachuting into enemy territory, scaling the world's highest peaks, or blasting off into space? Get to know the spies, adventure-seekers, and explorers in this chapter and it might be. They are just some of the women throughout history who've taken on some seriously dangerous missions, despite the risks. They've faced challenges that few, if any, had ever encountered before. Turn the page to plunge into their incredible stories.

Sarah McNair-Landry with sled dogs
on Baffin Island, Canada, in 2011

Amelia EARHART

FOR THIS GUTSY GAL, THE SKY WAS NO LIMIT

When Amelia Earhart made her mark on the world, women rarely held jobs outside the home. They were supposed to be wives and mothers; careers were for men. But Amelia was not one to conform to other people's expectations. She wore pants instead of dresses. She played football and fished. She read books and collected bugs. Above all, Amelia craved adventure.

SKY-HIGH DREAMS

When she was 23 years old, Amelia visited an air show and took her first airplane ride. It was only ten minutes long, but it changed her life forever. "By the time I had got two or three hundred feet [61 to 91 m] off the ground," she later said, "I knew I had to fly."

Less than two years after she began taking flying lessons, Amelia guided her plane to an altitude of 14,000 feet (4,267 m)—higher than any female pilot before her. She became the 16th woman to receive a pilot's license. She flew in races. And, in 1928, she became the first woman to fly across the Atlantic— though, to her disappointment, it was not as a pilot but as a passenger. Many people at that time thought the flight was too dangerous for a woman to be at the controls.

"ADVENTURE IS WORTHWHILE IN ITSELF."
—AMELIA EARHART

FEARLESS FACTS

BORN: July 24, 1897, Atchison, Kansas, U.S.A. **DISAPPEARED:** July 2, 1937, Pacific Ocean
OCCUPATION: Aviator **BOLDEST MOMENT:** Crossing the Atlantic solo

BREAKING BARRIERS

Though she later described her role on that first trans-Atlantic trip as "just baggage, like a sack of potatoes," the flight—and her book about the experience—made Amelia famous. She toured the country on a nationwide book tour. She encouraged women to break out of traditional female roles and study "male" subjects like engineering and medicine. She was already a celebrity, but her greatest accomplishment was still to come.

In 1932 she flew across the Atlantic again—this time, solo. She was the first woman—and only the second person in the world—ever to do so. Amelia said the flight proved that men and women were equal in "jobs requiring intelligence, coordination, speed, coolness, and willpower." After several more years of history-making solo flights and speed-breaking records, Amelia set her sights on attempting something no pilot—man or woman—had ever attempted before: to circle the globe around the equator.

INTO THIN AIR

In June 1937, after months of preparation, Amelia and her navigator, Fred Noonan, embarked on a long and dangerous journey around the world.

They took off from Florida, U.S.A., stopped in New Guinea, and then continued on. On July 2, 1937, while trying to locate Howland Island, in the Pacific, Amelia lost radio contact and vanished. Despite an exhaustive search, no trace of Amelia, Noonan, or her plane was found.

Since then, experts have made countless trips to small islands near where she went missing. They've discovered artifacts that some claim are evidence that Amelia crash-landed and survived for a time.

Nearly eight decades after her mysterious disappearance, Amelia still fascinates the world. For her guts and glory, her contributions to the history of flight, and her determination to succeed in what was regarded as a man's profession, Amelia Earhart is a heroine of the skies.

When people asked Amelia why she flew, she liked to say, "For the fun of it."

STRANDED: DID AMELIA EARHART SPEND HER FINAL DAYS AS A CASTAWAY?

Many think Earhart and her crashed craft were swallowed by the sea, never to be seen again. But others haven't managed to get the mystery of the missing aviator out of their minds. Members of the International Group for Historic Aircraft Recovery think Earhart and navigator Fred Noonan may have landed on a remote patch of land called Gardner Island and lived there as castaways. In 1940, the remains of a skeleton—judged to be most likely female—were discovered there, but the bones were tragically lost. More recently, researchers have found what could have been a campsite, with signs of past fires and thousands of bones from fish, turtles, and birds Earhart and Noonan may have caught, cooked, and eaten. Nearby were two buttons, pieces of a broken pocket-knife, and a cloth that appeared to have been shaped into a bow for hunting. Investigators also found a jar of freckle-lightening cream that the aviator—who was famously freckled—may have broken to create a cutting tool.

ONWARD AND UPWARD
PIONEERS OF AIR AND SPACE

In the early days of flight, crashes were common. But that didn't stop these female aviators and astronauts from trying to make their sky-high dreams come true. They broke records, stereotypes—and sometimes even the sound barrier. Along the way, they gave us heroines we could truly look up to.

LOFTY DREAM:
Baroness Raymonde de Laroche (1882–1919)

You'd never guess it from her name, but Baroness Raymonde de Laroche's family de-clogged toilets for a living. The Paris-born de Laroche pooh-poohed this career path and became the first woman in the world to get a pilot's license. She survived crash after crash, sometimes suffering injuries. But she always climbed back in the pilot's seat, until she reported to an airfield in Le Crotoy, France, to copilot an experimental plane. The craft crashed, killing de Laroche. If it had been successful, the flight would have made her the first female test pilot.

SPEED QUEEN: Jacqueline Cochran (1906–1980)

American aviator Jacqueline Cochran was one of the most influential pilots—man or woman—in the history of aviation. Born in a small mill town in Florida, U.S.A., she grew up with little education and was so poor that she didn't own a pair of shoes until she was nine. She went on to become a decorated pilot so famous that she was invited to dine with queens and presidents. Cochran was a natural-born flier, getting her pilot's license after only three weeks of lessons. Sometimes called the "Speed Queen," she set one racing record after another. Besides that, she was the first woman to break the sound barrier, the first woman to land and take off from an aircraft carrier, and the first woman to fly above 20,000 feet (6,096 m) without an oxygen mask. During World War II, she recruited and trained women to fly noncombat aircraft.

RIDE OF A LIFETIME: Dr. Sally Ride (1951–2012)

5-4-3-2-1... we have liftoff! On June 18, 1983, Sally Ride became the first American woman to travel to space. At 32, she was also the youngest astronaut to go to space, a record that stands today. While earning her Ph.D. in astrophysics at Stanford University in California, U.S.A., Ride had seen a newspaper ad calling for applicants to the astronaut program. Ride jumped at the chance. Since her barrier-breaking flight, 39 female NASA astronauts have blasted off into space. Ride went on to open doors for other women in science. In 2001, she founded Sally Ride Science, an organization that aims to inspire students—especially girls and minorities—to study the STEM subjects of science, technology, engineering, and math.

FIRST IN TRANSATLANTIC FLIGHT: Charles Lindbergh (1902–1974)

DARING DUDE

Airplane technology wasn't even a quarter of a century old in 1927, and soaring over vast stretches of empty ocean was risky in the days before satellite navigation. But daredevil pilot Charles Lindbergh was eager to make the first nonstop transatlantic flight all by himself. In May 1927, he took off from an airfield on Long Island, New York, U.S.A., in a plane called the *Spirit of St. Louis.* He flew through complete darkness, skimming the waves near Ireland to make sure he was still on course. Nearly 34 hours later, he landed at an airfield near Paris, France, where more than 100,000 people watched his historic landing. Lindbergh's flight set the stage for modern long-distance air travel. A flight from New York to Paris today takes less than eight hours.

BOLD ENDEAVOUR: Dr. Mae Jemison (1956–)

When a kindergarten teacher asked Mae Jemison what she wanted to be when she grew up, young Mae replied, "A scientist." The teacher was surprised; there weren't very many female scientists at the time, and almost none were African American. But a determined Mae studied chemical engineering, became a medical doctor, and applied to NASA to be an astronaut. When the space shuttle *Endeavour* launched into orbit in 1992, Jemison became the first African-American woman in space.

Jessica WATSON

SOLO SAILOR

Jessica Watson was a shy and quiet kid growing up in Queensland, Australia—not the kind of girl who seemed destined for adventure. But when she was 11, she heard the story of Jesse Martin, who in 1999 had sailed around the world solo at age 18 and set the record for the youngest person to make the trip. Jessica was inspired. She decided that she, too, wanted to sail around the globe. And she would make the trip unassisted—meaning that once she was out there, no one could help her.

It took Jessica five years to prepare for the journey. She had to learn about how to sail on the ocean, how to guide her boat through stormy weather, how to navigate, how to repair her craft, and how to perform first aid on herself in case she got injured. On October 18, 2009, the 16-year-old sailed her pink craft out of Australia's Sydney Harbor and into her great adventure.

During her seven-month voyage, Jessica faced danger many times. One storm in the Atlantic rolled her boat over four times. And a wave picked her boat up when it was completely upside down and threw it on top of the next wave rolling in. "There wasn't a lot I could do," Jessica said, "Except hunker down ... and stand on the ceiling." She also saw incredible sights, like a shooting star racing across the night sky and magnificent sunrises on the open ocean.

After more than half a year alone at sea, Jessica sailed back into Sydney Harbor after successfully circling the globe. She is the youngest person to have accomplished an around-the-world solo sail.

> "I DON'T CONSIDER MYSELF A HERO. I'M AN ORDINARY GIRL WHO BELIEVED IN HER DREAM."
> —JESSICA WATSON

FEARLESS FACTS

➲ **BORN:** May 18, 1993, Gold Coast, Australia ➲ **OCCUPATION:** Sailor ➲ **BOLDEST MOMENT:** Circling the globe solo at the age of 16

Jeanne BARET

FIRST WOMAN TO CIRCLE THE GLOBE

Jeanne Baret was born in 1740 in Autun, France. Even though she was a peasant, she became an herb woman, an expert in botanical medicine who knew which leaves and flowers could treat wounds and diseases. One day, she made friends with Philibert de Commerson, another plant expert. Two years later, de Commerson got the job offer of a lifetime: The French government was sending two ships around the world to discover new land, and they wanted de Commerson onboard to find new plants. He wanted to bring his plant-hunting partner Baret along—but the French Navy did not allow women on its ships. What was the duo to do?

Baret decided to sneak aboard in plain sight—dressed as a man. For a year, she successfully kept her secret safe and hunted plants with de Commerson. Eventually, however, some of the crew started to get suspicious. They confronted Baret, and her secret identity was revealed. The captain ordered her off the ship in Mauritius, an island in East Africa.

Years later, she sailed back to where she had begun her journey in France. In doing so, she completed a circuit of the globe. When she glided into port, there was no one cheering. Her name didn't appear in any news headlines. Baret herself probably wasn't aware of what she had done. But she had done it all the same: She was the first woman to have sailed all the way around the world.

BARET BOARDED THE SHIP DRESSED AS A MAN—AND KEPT HER SECRET SAFE FOR A YEAR.

FEARLESS FACTS

➡ **BORN:** July 27, 1740, Autun, France ➡ **DIED:** August 5, 1807, Saint-Aulaye, France
➡ **OCCUPATION:** Botanist ➡ **BOLDEST MOMENT:** Becoming the first woman to sail around the world

ON THE FRONT LINES
RISKING LIFE AND LIMB

It wasn't until 2016 that the U.S. Armed Services gave women official permission to serve in front-line combat units. But that wasn't the first time in history women had joined the fight. Meet four incredible females who put it all on the line for what they thought was right.

SAMURAI SHERO: Nakano Takeko (1847–1868)

Japanese warrior Nakano Takeko was an expert in martial arts almost from the time she could walk. So when the Japanese civil war, or the Boshin War, broke out in 1868, she was ready to fight. As a woman, Takeko couldn't join the official army—so she created her own.

Takeko led an all-female army of samurai soldiers later dubbed the Women's Army. These fierce females' weapon of choice was the naginata—a pole with a curved blade at the end. The naginata gave its wielders a long reach as they faced off with men in battle, making up for the women's smaller size.

While leading a charge against enemy forces, Takeko was fatally wounded, and she died on the battlefield. Today, a monument stands on the spot, and every year, the people of Japan honor Takeko and her brave band of female fighters.

GUERILLA GIRL: Nancy Wake (1912–2011)

In the mid-1930s, New Zealand–born journalist Nancy Wake was working as a European correspondent in Vienna, Austria, when she saw gangs of Nazis savagely beating Jewish men and women in the streets. She promised herself that if she could ever do anything to stop the Nazis, she would.

When the Nazis invaded France in 1940, Wake got her chance. She risked life and limb to smuggle British soldiers and citizens out of the country, saving hundreds of lives. This work put her life constantly in danger; at one point, she was number one on the most-wanted list of the Gestapo—Nazi secret police—with a five-million-franc (5.2-million-dollar) bounty on her head. But that didn't stop Wake. She parachuted into Normandy before D-Day and planted weapons for Allied soldiers. The Gestapo tried to catch her, but she always stayed one step ahead of them. They nicknamed her the White Mouse for her ability to evade capture.

BOND, JANE BOND: Eileen Nearne (1921–2010)

After World War II broke out, Eileen Nearne volunteered for one of the most dangerous jobs in the British military: secret agent. In 1944, Nearne—code-name Agent Rose—parachuted into Nazi-occupied France to help the French Resistance, groups of citizens who used guerrilla tactics (like ambushes, raids, and hit-and-runs) to weaken the German forces. Nearne operated a top secret radio link between France and Britain, relaying messages about Nazi activities and organizing weapons drops to the resistance fighters.

On July 25, 1944, the Gestapo discovered Nearne's hideout. She quickly burned her messages and hid her radio, but they found it anyway. They arrested her and took her to Gestapo headquarters. There, they tortured her until she nearly died. But Nearne didn't break. She managed to persuade her captors that she had been sending messages for a businessman, who she didn't know was British. The Gestapo sent her from one concentration camp to another, where she worked 12 hours a day building roads. While being transported on April 9, 1945, Nearne escaped, sleeping in the woods and hiding in a church belfry until she reached American troops. She lived to be 89, largely in private and out of the public eye.

THE GIRL WHO LED AN ARMY: Joan of Arc
(ca 1412–1431)

When she was 13 years old, Joan of Arc began hearing voices in her head. She was convinced that they belonged to saints—St. Michael, St. Catherine, and St. Margaret—and that they spoke messages from God.

At that time, the English had taken over France, and the voices were telling Joan that she had to help win back her country's land. The voices instructed Joan to cut her hair and dress in men's clothing. Disguised, she traveled more than 300 miles (480 km) in May 1428 to see the French king, Charles VII. When she got to his castle, Joan relayed her holy message. Though she was just a child, she must have made a convincing case: Charles VII sent his soldiers into battle against the English, with Joan alongside to boost morale. Filled with religious righteousness, the French Army beat its enemy into retreat in the Battle of Orléans.

Later, English soldiers captured Joan, accused her of using witchcraft, and burned her at the stake. She was just 19 years old. Modern doctors think that she may have had a medical condition that made her hear voices. But whatever the reason for her actions, she was one courageous girl. Joan was declared a saint in 1920, and the French still celebrate her bravery today.

Conquering
THE SEVEN

In the northern mountains of Nepal, the snow-capped peak of Mount Everest dwarfs the landscape around it. At 29,029 feet (8,848 m), it is the highest mountain above sea level in the world. Climbers journey to Nepal from around the globe to fulfill their dreams of reaching its summit. To date, about 240 people have died in the attempt. With earthquakes, avalanches, and storms that can come without warning—not to mention the threats of climbing accidents and the dangers of altitude sickness—Everest is one of the most dangerous climbs on Earth.

Half of the 4,000 climbers who have ventured up Everest's treacherous slopes are from Nepal—but only two dozen of them have been women; it's usually the men who get the chance to climb. One group of seven women from Nepal decided to set out to conquer Everest and show their country—and the world—that climbing isn't just a sport for men.

The climbers, from left: Maya Gurung, Nimdoma Sherpa, Chunu Shrestha, Pema Dikki, Asha Kumari Singh, Shailee Basnet, and Pujan Acharya

SUMMITS

AN **ALL-FEMALE TEAM** CLIMBS THE HIGHEST MOUNTAIN ON EACH CONTINENT

The young group started training in 2007. Their legs burned as they ran mile after mile; their arms ached as they scaled climbing walls. Some had to train in secret so their families wouldn't find out.

When the girls reached Everest base camp in 2008, conditions were even worse than they had anticipated: the temperatures were colder, the air much thinner. The other climbers at base camp were older, taller, and more experienced. The group of girls didn't look like they belonged: One of their members, Nimdoma Sherpa, was only four feet ten inches (1.5 m) tall and 17 years old. The experienced climbers didn't think the girls would get to the top. Some of them even made bets on how many of them would die.

But the group pushed ahead, climbing five to ten hours a day, telling jokes and singing songs when they felt too cold to go on. On May 22, 2008, the first members of the team reached the summit. When they set foot on Earth's highest peak, a few of these awe-inspiring explorers broke records: Maya Gurung and Asha Kumari Singh became the first women from their villages to make the climb, and Nimdoma became the youngest woman ever.

The climbers met with U.S. secretary of state John Kerry in 2014.

Team leader Shailee Basnet looks at climbing gear at a store in Katmandu, Nepal.

After Everest, the team decided they weren't done yet. They set their sights on the Seven Summits, the highest mountains on each continent. Though only 400 people in the world have conquered the Seven Summits—not one of them a Nepalese woman—the girls decided to go for it anyway. Over the next six years, they took on the treacherous mountains one by one. On December 23, 2015, they reached the top of the final peak, Mount Vinson Massif in Antarctica, becoming the first all-female team to complete the feat. They showed their country—and the world—that women have the physical and mental strength necessary to tackle one of mountaineering's toughest challenges.

Sacagawea

CHARTING A COURSE INTO HISTORY

Imagine a teenager, just 16 or 17 years old, guiding a group of men through wild territory. Along the way, she leads them through a place she hasn't seen since she was 11 or 12. And she does it all while caring for her two-month-old baby. This bold adventurer was a real woman named Sacagawea, the only female member of the Lewis and Clark expedition.

EXPLORER ENCOUNTER

Sacagawea was the daughter of a Native American chief who grew up surrounded by the Rocky Mountains in what is now Idaho, U.S.A. Her tribe, the Shoshone, had fearsome enemies: the Hidatsa tribe. When Sacagawea was just 12 years old, the Hidatsa captured her and sold her to a French-Canadian fur trader named Toussaint Charbonneau, who made Sacagawea his wife. Around the same time, U.S. president Thomas Jefferson was signing on the dotted line to make the Louisiana Purchase—828,000 square miles (2,144,510 sq km) that formed the middle of the United States. Nobody knew what lay inside that land, only that it was wild territory. Jefferson appointed two men to find out: Meriwether Lewis and William Clark. Today, they are known as famous explorers, but they may not have made it back alive if not for Sacagawea.

> WITHOUT SACAGAWEA'S COOL HEAD AND NAVIGATIONAL SKILLS, THE FAMOUS LEWIS AND CLARK EXPEDITION COULD HAVE ENDED IN DISASTER.

FEARLESS FACTS

● **BORN:** ca 1788, Salmon, Idaho, U.S.A. ● **DIED:** ca 1812, Kenel, South Dakota, U.S.A. ● **OCCUPATION:** Interpreter and navigator ● **BOLDEST MOMENT:** Saving the Lewis and Clark expedition

SETTING OUT

On November 2, 1804, Lewis and Clark reached Sacagawea's settlement near present-day Bismarck, South Dakota, where they met Sacagawea and Charbonneau. When the explorers realized the couple could speak several Native American languages between them, they knew they'd be the perfect translators for the trip and asked them to come along.

Young Sacagawea strapped her newborn son to her back and set out for adventure. She was the only woman to travel with the 33 members of the expedition all the way to the Pacific Ocean and back, and she proved herself to be one of the team's most valuable members. In addition to her skills as a translator, she could identify plants that could be used for food and medicine. And when the group encountered Native American tribes—some of whom had never seen a white person before—Sacagawea's presence let them know the explorers came in peace: War parties didn't travel with women.

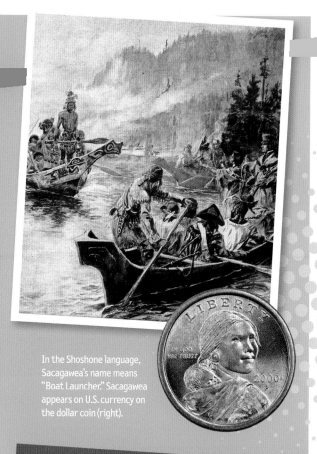

In the Shoshone language, Sacagawea's name means "Boat Launcher." Sacagawea appears on U.S. currency on the dollar coin (right).

SACAGAWEA SAVES THE DAY

The explorers were traveling down the Missouri River on May 14, 1805, when one of their boats was hit by a high wind and nearly capsized. Papers, books, navigational instruments, and medicines—along with journals documenting the first year of their journey—started to float away. The boat's crew panicked, but Sacagawea didn't. She calmly fished the items out of the river before they could float away, saving them—and the mission.

After the crew reached the Pacific, the party set off on the return trip, passing through Sacagawea's homeland. Though she hadn't been in the territory for years, she remembered the Shoshone trails of her childhood and became the party's guide, leading them through that untamed territory.

On August 14, 1806, after 16 months in the wilderness, the Lewis and Clark party made it back to their starting point. On their 8,000-mile (12,875-km) journey they had survived hunger, mosquito swarms, illness, and extreme weather. Without Sacagawea, the famous expedition would likely have been lost to history.

HEROIC EXPLORERS: LEWIS AND CLARK

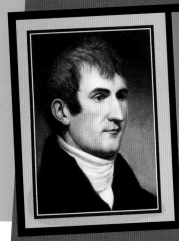

DARING DUDE

When Thomas Jefferson sent Lewis and Clark out to explore the unknown West, he thought they might find woolly mammoths and volcanoes spewing lava skyward. Jefferson was wrong about the details, but Lewis and Clark did make astonishing discoveries. They found 300 plant and animal species that were completely new to science at the time, as well as unexpected geography, including the Rocky Mountains. The maps they made of the uncharted territory helped pioneers settle the new frontier.

DRESSED AS A MAN
THEY SWAPPED SKIRTS FOR PANTS

When these gutsy gals were told "No girls allowed," they found a way to do it anyway. The women on these pages went to great lengths to disguise themselves—one even splashed her face with disinfectant to get a leathery "masculine" look! The only thing they couldn't hide? How tough they were.

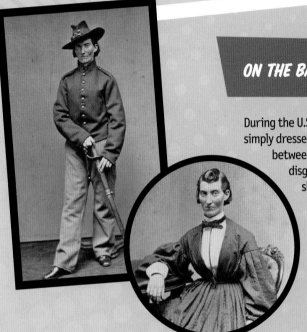

ON THE BATTLEFIELD: Frances Clayton (ca 1830–?)

During the U.S. Civil War, women weren't allowed to join the army. So, many simply dressed as men and went off to war anyway! Historians estimate that between 150 and 400 Civil War soldiers were actually women in disguise. One of them was Frances Clayton. Clayton cut her hair short, put on men's clothing, and practiced walking, talking, and chewing tobacco like a soldier. She enlisted in the Union Army as "Jack Williams" and fought by her husband's side in 18 battles. A skirmish at Stones River in December 1892 ended with Clayton wounded, and her husband was killed. She might have kept fighting, but the bullet in her hip sent her to the hospital, where her deception was finally discovered.

PIRATE QUEEN: Anne Bonny (ca 1698–ca 1782)

It was an old sailor's saying that a woman on a ship brought bad luck. But not if the ship was a pirate ship and the woman was Anne Bonny.

The Irish-born Bonny fell in love with a pirate named John "Calico Jack" Rackham and joined his crew for a life on the high seas. Legend says she began her pirating career by cleverly tricking a passing merchant ship into giving up its goods by using a fake corpse she'd made with a mannequin and some fake blood. When the ship's crew saw Bonny standing over her "victim," they surrendered without a fight. Most of the time, Bonny dressed as a woman. But she found that skirts got in the way of pillaging and plundering, so when it was time for piracy, she would forgo her dresses for pants.

WOMAN MARINE: Hannah Snell (1723–1792)

Born in Worcester, England, Hannah Snell wed a Dutch sailor when she was 20 and thought she would settle down into married life. When her husband abandoned her after a few months, Snell was furious. She borrowed a man's suit from her brother-in-law James Grey, took on his name, and set off to hunt down her missing spouse dressed as a soldier. She kept up the search—and her disguise—for five years. During that time, she served in the Royal Marines, sailing to India through terrible storms and sustaining more than a dozen wounds. In 1750, her ship returned to England, where Snell revealed her true identity. Her story created a sensation, and in later years, Snell wrote an autobiography about her adventures and opened a pub called the Female Warrior.

FRONTLINE FEMALE: Dorothy Lawrence (1896–1964)

British-born Dorothy Lawrence wanted to be a journalist during World War I—and she wanted to tell her stories from the front lines. She decided that the only way to get there was in disguise. She built a homemade corset to flatten her curves, chopped off her long hair, and used a chemical disinfectant to make her skin look weathered. Lawrence traveled toward the battlefields of Somme, France. She joined the ranks of the 179 Tunneling Company, soldiers who were digging underground to the German lines to plant bombs. Wracked with worry she would be discovered, Lawrence finally confessed to the commanding officer. She was forced to sign a document saying that she wouldn't write about her experiences, dashing her journalistic dream.

WILD WEST: Charley Parkhurst (1812–1879)

Driving a stagecoach was one of the most dangerous jobs in the Old West. Stagecoach drivers had to negotiate primitive trails and fight off bandits, all while controlling a team of up to six horses. But the job wasn't too tough for Charley Parkhurst. Also known as Six-Horse Charley or One-Eyed Charley (after losing the use of an eye to a horse kick), she posed as a man and earned a reputation as one of the finest stagecoach drivers around. It wasn't until Parkhurst's death that the secret came out: The daring driver had been a woman!

Gertrude BELL

DESERT DAME

Writer, world traveler, spy, explorer, archaeologist, political officer, shaper of nations: Gertrude Bell did it all—and she did it at a time when these adventures were the realm of men.

At the age of 19, the British-born Bell became the first female to complete a first-class honors degree in modern history at the University of Oxford. But because she was a woman, she wasn't allowed to graduate. Bell shrugged off the setback and set off to see what the world was like outside of England. She took a trip to Iran, where she became fascinated with the Middle East—an interest that would shape the rest of her life.

In 1899, Bell once again traveled to the Middle East and, for more than a decade, crisscrossed the desert making maps of uncharted regions. She often journeyed alone, once going 1,500 miles (2,414 km) across central Arabia by camel. She knew the region so well that when one important Iraqi leader was asked about where the border of his land was, he referred his questioner to Bell.

During World War I, the British intelligence unit asked Bell to become a spy, using her knowledge of the Middle East to forge alliances with Arab tribes. When the British took over Baghdad in 1917, Bell helped design a new state called Iraq. She crafted its constitution, put leaders in place, and drew its borders. Her writings on the politics of the Middle East are still studied today.

> "IT'S SO NICE TO BE A SPOKE IN THE WHEEL, ONE THAT HELPS TO TURN, NOT ONE THAT HINDERS."
> —GERTRUDE BELL

FEARLESS FACTS

→ **BORN:** July 14, 1868, Durham, England → **DIED:** July 12, 1926, Baghdad, Iraq
→ **OCCUPATION:** Adventurer, political officer, archaeologist, spy → **BOLDEST MOMENT:** Being a diplomatic dame among dudes

Gertrude EDERLE

CHANNEL CHAMP

Crossing the English Channel—the body of water that separates England from France—is often called the Everest of Swimming. The Channel is a tough, dangerous passage, with water that often dips below 50°F (10°C) and is booby-trapped with unpredictable currents that can double the 21-mile (34-km) swimming distance.

Before 1923, only five men had successfully made the swim. So when 19-year-old Gertrude Ederle conquered the Channel in 1926—and beat all their time records doing it—she shocked the world.

Ederle was a champion swimmer her whole life, setting records and competing in the Olympics through the 1920s. She first attempted to swim the Channel in 1925. After she had gone 23 miles (37 km), the people in her support boat thought she was drowning and reached out to help her, disqualifying her swim. Ederle hadn't been drowning—only resting—and she was distraught. She vowed to try again, and this time, she made her team promise not to touch her, no matter how bad she looked.

Just after 7 a.m. on August 6, 1926, Ederle waded into the Channel at Cape Gris-Nez, France. On the shore was a red ball, a warning to boats to avoid the choppy water. "Please, God, help me," she said. Fourteen hours and 31 minutes later—a world record—Ederle stumbled ashore in Kingsdown, England. The sea had been so rough that swimming against the current had added distance to her trip. In the end, she had swum at least 35 miles (56 km). Her record remained unbroken for 24 years.

"I JUST KNEW IF IT COULD BE DONE, IT HAD TO BE DONE, AND I DID IT."
—GERTRUDE EDERLE

FEARLESS FACTS

➲ **BORN:** October 23, 1905, New York, New York, U.S.A. ➲ **DIED:** November 20, 2003, Wyckoff, New Jersey, U.S.A. ➲ **OCCUPATION:** Swimmer ➲ **BOLDEST MOMENT:** Becoming the first woman to swim the English Channel

MOMENT OF BRAVERY

When adventure turned into misadventure, would this daring dogsledder find the guts to keep pushing forward?

THE SITUATION

On February 1, 2015, Sarah McNair-Landry set off on the trip of a lifetime. She and her boyfriend, Erik Boomer, were going to circle Canada's snowy Baffin Island by dogsled, retracing a route McNair-Landry's parents had taken 25 years before. With its extremely cold climate and year-round snows, Baffin Island is one of the wildest places on Earth. The journey around the 195,928-square-mile (507,451-sq-km) island—the fifth largest in the world—would take four months. But just four days in, something went wrong.

The dogsledding duo was moving across a high plateau when a big storm blew in. There was nothing to protect them from the screaming 56-mile-an-hour (90-km/h) winds. The dogs—unwilling to run face-first into the gusts—started to rebel. They turned and bolted. The lines looped around McNair-Landry's foot, and the next thing she knew, she was being dragged under the sled at high speed.

THE MOMENT OF TRUTH

As quickly as he could, Boomer got the dogs under control, and McNair-Landry crawled out from under the sled, unharmed but dazed. For a few horrible moments while trapped under the sled, she had thought she was going to break her leg—or worse—in the middle of the wilderness. There were thousands of miles left to go on this treacherous journey, and no guarantees that she'd get as lucky if another accident struck. But McNair-Landry didn't turn tail and head for home. She and Boomer pushed ahead. On June 2, 2015, they returned safely to their starting point of Iqaluit, Nunavut—McNair-Landry's hometown—successfully completing their journey after 120 days in the frigid Canadian Arctic.

THE LEGACY

McNair-Landry's tale is an inspiration, but it was just one chapter in a life of epic adventures. She grew up with the Arctic Ocean and a team of dogs in her backyard. When she turned 18, she became the youngest person to ski to the South Pole. Then, in 2006, she dogsledded to the North Pole—becoming the youngest person to reach both poles. She's also kayaked 450 miles (724 km) across the Sea of Cortez and piloted a three-wheeled buggy across Mongolia's Gobi desert.

In 2007, McNair-Landry was awarded National Geographic's Adventurer of the Year, and she's continued to live up to that title. In 2011, she and her brother kite-skied more than 2,000 miles (3,219 km) through the Canadian Arctic. They fended off polar bears and faced some of the coldest, windiest conditions on Earth. McNair-Landry documents her expeditions on film, inspiring the next generation of explorers.

Peace HEROINES

Some of the bravest women and girls in history wielded words and wisdom instead of weapons. These peacemakers fought for truth, justice, and equal rights; crusaded for better living conditions and better opportunities for people in poverty; faced threats and even grave danger to get an education; and endured persecution for speaking out for what was right. Read on for their astounding stories of hope, tenacity, and courage.

Malala Yousafzai speaks in
Birmingham, England, in 2015.

Harriet TUBMAN

SAVIOR OF SLAVES

Harriet Tubman was born a slave in Maryland's Dorchester County around 1820. When her owner died in 1849, Tubman was afraid that she would be sold and her family torn apart. She decided instead to escape.

The journey north to freedom was so dangerous that most slaves didn't dare attempt it. But Tubman did—and she made it to the free state of Pennsylvania. Once there, however, she didn't stay safe for long. Tubman headed back to the South to bring her family to freedom—the first of many return trips she would make. Rescuing slaves became her life's mission.

PATH TO FREEDOM

Growing up as a slave, Harriet Tubman endured physical violence as part of her everyday life. Once, as a teenager, she was running an errand when she came across a slave who had left the fields without permission. The man's overseer told Harriet to help stop the runaway. When she said no, the overseer threw a two-pound (0.9-kg) weight at Harriet's head, causing seizures and severe headaches that would plague her for a lifetime.

"EVERY GREAT DREAM BEGINS WITH A DREAMER."
—HARRIET TUBMAN

FEARLESS FACTS

➔ **BORN:** ca 1822, Dorchester County, Maryland, U.S.A. ➔ **DIED:** March 10, 1913, Auburn, New York, U.S.A.
➔ **OCCUPATION:** Abolitionist ➔ **BOLDEST MOMENT:** Guiding slaves to freedom

Tubman never forgot the horrors she endured. Her desire to save others from the same terrible fate drove her to become a guide, or conductor, on the Underground Railroad, a network of secret routes and houses where slaves could hide on the perilous journey northward. Runaways had to travel great distances, often on foot and with very little food to eat. They had to cross treacherous rivers and fend off wild animals. Burrs from the forests' sweet gum trees would slice open their feet. And they were often just a few steps ahead of slave catchers intent on chasing them down for reward money. If runaways were caught, they would be beaten, branded, jailed, or even killed.

UNDERGROUND HERO

Tubman's actions earned her many enemies in the South. By 1856, Maryland planters offered a $40,000 reward for Tubman's capture. But even that couldn't stop her. Tubman used clever tricks to get her precious cargo to the safety of the North. She liked to give her party an advantage over slave hunters by starting their journey on a Saturday night, because she knew notices reporting a slave's escape wouldn't appear in the newspapers until Monday. When she encountered slave owners while on the road, she would turn around and pretend to be heading south.

By 1860, she had made the trip to slave country and back an astonishing 13 times. She even rescued her 70-year-old parents, whose age made the journey especially challenging. All told, she helped free about 70 slaves through the Underground Railroad and was proud to say that she never lost one along the way. When the Civil War began in 1861, Tubman joined the fight, leading a raid to free more than 700 slaves in South Carolina. Abolitionist John Brown called her General Tubman, once saying she was "one of the bravest persons on this continent." She died surrounded by friends and family members at age 91.

Tubman earned the nickname Moses, after the biblical prophet who led his people to freedom.

RIGHTS FOR ALL: Frederick Douglass (ca 1818–1895)

DARING DUDE

Former slave Frederick Douglass was most famous for his crusade as a leader of the abolitionist movement. But Douglass believed that the fight for equality didn't end with freeing slaves. He was also a supporter of women's rights, writing, "Right is of no sex, truth is of no color." In 1848, he was one of the few men present at the first Women's Rights Convention in Seneca Falls, New York, U.S.A. Famous suffragettes Susan B. Anthony and Elizabeth Cady Stanton worked with Douglass to create the American Equal Rights Association in 1866. They demanded that everyone in America be allowed the right to vote.

THEY RISKED IT ALL
FIGHTING FOR JUSTICE

Changing the world can start with something as simple as signing a petition or attending a meeting. These society shakers did that, but they didn't stop there. They battled bravely for what they believed in—and laid their reputations, their careers, and even their lives on the line to do it.

FREEDOM FIGHTERS:
Sarah and Angelina Grimke
(1792–1873) and (1805–1879)

Born into a wealthy family in Charleston, South Carolina, U.S.A., Sarah and Angelina Grimke were destined for a life of luxury. They could have spent their days attending the balls and dinner parties of Charleston's elite society, with slaves taking care of their every need. But the Grimke sisters shunned their lives of wealth and ease. In 1827, they moved to Pennsylvania, where the antislavery movement was just beginning. They became abolitionists (people who worked to end slavery) and feminists (people who work for women's equality). They wrote letters and gave speeches to support freedom for all. The Grimke sisters endured hatred for their actions. An angry mob once threw stones at the windows of a building where Angelina was speaking at an antislavery convention and then came back the next day to ransack the building and set it on fire. But that didn't stop the Grimke sisters—they kept up the fight their entire lives.

AWE-INSPIRING ACTIVIST:
Rigoberta Menchú Tum (1959–)

Indigenous, or native, people in the Americas have struggled against racism for centuries. In Rigoberta Menchú Tum's home country of Guatemala, the military dictatorship severely repressed indigenous people. In the late 1970s, Tum's mother, father, and brother were all killed by the Guatemalan Army. Even though she knew she could easily share her family's fate, Tum protested the human rights abuses she was witnessing. Death threats forced her to flee Guatemala several times. In 1983, she wrote a book called I, Rigoberta Menchú that brought the world's attention to the story of her people. In 1992, she won the Nobel Peace Prize—becoming the first indigenous person to ever be honored with the award.

PEACEFUL PROTESTER: Rosa Parks (1913–2005)

Rosa Parks is famous for refusing to give up her bus seat to a white passenger on December 1, 1955. But her story didn't stop there. As a result of her refusal, Parks was arrested for violating the laws of segregation that kept blacks and whites separate. When she was tried and found guilty, the injustice sparked a protest. Forty thousand African-American commuters in Montgomery, Alabama, U.S.A., banded together and refused to use the bus system, most walking to work instead—some going as far as 20 miles (32 km) on foot. The movement, known as the Montgomery Bus Boycott, was the first large-scale protest against segregation. It continued for more than a year, with the city of Montgomery losing thousands of dollars each day. The boycott brought national attention to racial segregation in the South and spurred the U.S. Supreme Court to rule in 1956 that bus segregation was unconstitutional. Parks was fired from her job, and she and her husband had to leave Alabama in 1957 because of threats to their safety. But Parks continued to work for civil rights for the rest of her life. Her act of courage helped spur the beginning of the civil rights movement in the United States and became a symbol of the fight for equality.

RADICAL REPORTER: Nellie Bly (1864–1922)

When Elizabeth Jane Cochran was 18, she read something in a Pittsburgh, Pennsylvania, U.S.A., newspaper column that made her angry. It said that women belonged inside the home performing domestic duties and that those who worked outside the home were "a monstrosity." Elizabeth penned a response so spirited that the newspaper offered her a job—along with the pen name Nellie Bly.

Investigative reporting became Bly's passion. But when her editors kept assigning her stories for the women's page, she left Pittsburgh and headed for New York. After half a year trying to find a reporting job, an editor at the *New York World* asked her to write about an institution for the mentally ill. To get the inside story, Bly pretended to be sick so she could be committed and experience the treatment of a patient firsthand. The groundbreaking 1887 exposé she wrote shed light on how truly cruel and awful the conditions were, prompting much-needed reform of the hospital. Bly was a pioneer of the field of investigative journalism and an early advocate for women's rights.

THE ULTIMATE SACRIFICE: Harvey Milk (1930–1978)

DARING DUDE

During the early years of his life, while serving as a diver in the U.S. Navy in the Korean War and working as a public school teacher in New York, U.S.A., Harvey Milk kept a secret: He was gay. If he let his secret slip, he risked becoming the target of hate. Milk's outlook changed when he moved to San Francisco in 1972 and saw his gay friends being harassed by police. In 1977, Milk entered politics, winning a position on the San Francisco Board of Supervisors and becoming one of the first openly gay officials in the United States. He helped pass a city law that outlawed discrimination based on sexual orientation. Tragically, Milk was shot and killed in 1978 by an angry former San Francisco supervisor.

Mother TERESA

CARED FOR THOSE IN NEED

As a young girl in Skopje, Macedonia, Mother Teresa (born Agnes Bojaxhiu) was fascinated with the lives of missionaries—members of religious groups who journey to far-flung areas to spread their faith. By age 12, Agnes decided that she too would spend her life serving her religion. She became a nun at age 18 and was sent to Calcutta, India (now called Kolkata), where she witnessed events that changed the course of her life.

In 1943, a famine struck southern Asia, and three million people died of starvation. Then, in 1946, riots erupted when two religious groups, Hindus and Muslims, savagely attacked each other. These devastating events hit Calcutta's massive poor population the hardest. The suffering Mother Teresa witnessed made a deep impression on her. In 1948, she went to live among Calcutta's poorest. In a show of respect to those she served, she donned a traditional blue and white Indian sari, which she would wear for the rest of her life.

For many years, Mother Teresa and a small group of her fellow nuns lived on just enough income and food to survive—they often had to beg for funds. But slowly, Mother Teresa's work began to gain supporters. In 1952, she turned an abandoned Hindu temple into a place that cared for those in need at the end of their lives. She also extended her charitable work to helping the blind, orphans, the disabled, and the aged. In 1979, Mother Teresa was awarded the Nobel Peace Prize.

FEW FIGURES HAVE BEEN AS BELOVED ACROSS THE WORLD.

FEARLESS FACTS

➔ **BORN:** August 26, 1910, Skopje, Macedonia ➔ **DIED:** September 5, 1997, Calcutta, India
➔ **OCCUPATION:** Nun, missionary ➔ **BOLDEST MOMENT:** Devoting her life to those in need

Jane ADDAMS

BETTERED LIVES AND COMMUNITIES

Jane Addams was born into a wealthy family in Cedarville, Illinois, U.S.A., with society's most powerful people—including President Abraham Lincoln—as family friends. Addams was among the first generation of American women to attend college, graduating in 1881 from Rockford Female Seminary. But after her privileged start in life, Addams struggled to find her place in the world.

At the age of 27, Addams and her friend Ellen Gates Starr traveled to London, England, to visit Toynbee Hall, a settlement house. It was a charitable organization that provided adult education classes, after-school kids' programs, senior care, and other community services for a disadvantaged community. Inspired by the difference Toynbee Hall made in people's lives, Addams had found her life's mission. She and Starr would go back home and open a settlement house of their own in one of Chicago's struggling neighborhoods.

Addams and Starr moved into a large home built by a man named Charles Hull. They held rallies and made speeches about the needs of the neighborhood, raised money, and persuaded others to join their cause. Two years later, Hull-House was hosting 2,000 people every week. It had a kindergarten for children, club meetings for teens, and night classes for adults. As Hull-House grew, it added an art gallery, a music school, a library, and more.

Addams became a social reformer, an advocate for world peace, and—in the days before women were even allowed to vote—an outspoken feminist. In 1931, she was awarded the Nobel Peace Prize, the first American woman ever to earn the honor.

> "NOTHING COULD BE WORSE THAN THE FEAR THAT ONE HAD GIVEN UP TOO SOON, AND LEFT ONE UNEXPENDED EFFORT THAT MIGHT HAVE SAVED THE WORLD."
> —JANE ADDAMS

FEARLESS FACTS

➔ **BORN:** September 6, 1860, Cedarville, Illinois, U.S.A. ➔ **DIED:** May 21, 1935, Chicago, Illinois, U.S.A.
➔ **OCCUPATION:** Activist, author, lecturer, community organizer ➔ **BOLDEST MOMENT:** Making it her mission to help the less fortunate

GIRL POWER
WOMEN'S RIGHTS CHAMPIONS

In the early 1800s, American women were treated as second-class citizens. They weren't supposed to get an education or pursue a career, and they weren't allowed to own property, keep their own wages, sign a contract ... or even vote! Meet the women who championed a 70-year movement to change all that.

EQUALITY CRUSADER: Susan B. Anthony (1820–1906)

Susan B. Anthony was working as a teacher in Canajoharie, New York, U.S.A., earning $2.50 a month, when she discovered something upsetting: Male teachers at her school were earning $10 a month. The revelation sparked Anthony's lifelong fight for equality for women. She handed out pamphlets and made speeches campaigning for women's rights to own property and vote in elections. In 1872, Anthony decided to take direct action and voted illegally in a presidential election. She was arrested and convicted of a crime, but she refused to pay the fine in protest.

Anthony believed that everyone, not just women, should be treated fairly. She worked to pass labor laws protecting workers and an amendment to the U.S. Constitution outlawing slavery. In her more than 50 years of social reform, Anthony was laughed out of Congress, arrested, and threatened by hostile mobs. But she was tireless and, ultimately, successful. In 1920, 11 years after her death, the 19th Amendment—also known as the Susan B. Anthony Amendment—gave women the right to vote.

FAMOUS FEMINIST: Gloria Steinem (1934–)

When she started working as a freelance magazine writer, Gloria Steinem wanted to pen stories about serious subjects like politics. But her editors wouldn't assign those articles to a woman. Instead, they made her write about fashion, makeup, and babies. So Steinem quit journalism to become an activist, giving speeches and writing essays about how women were not being treated equally in America. In 1971, she worked with other prominent feminists to form the National Women's

PINK LADIES: The Gulabi Gang

In Banda, one of India's most poverty-stricken districts, women have historically been treated as second-class citizens. Political corruption has always run rampant, abuse of women by men is not uncommon, and the police force has not done much to help.

In 2006, one group of women decided to take justice into their own hands. The Gulabi Gang, as they call themselves, are more than 10,000 strong. Every day nearly half a dozen women travel to the group's unofficial headquarters in a small pink house in the town of Badausa to ask for help. Many of these women have to take long and dangerous journeys to get there, traveling on rickety buses or hitchhiking on unsafe roads. When members of the Gulabi Gang hear the story of an oppressed woman who needs their assistance, the ladies—clad in pink saris—take action to combat the violence, sometimes carrying lathis (traditional Indian fighting sticks) for protection, in case their opponents resort to force. The gang stands up for many women in India who have no other protectors.

UNITING A MOVEMENT:
Emma Watson (1990–)

Known for her starring role as brave and brainy Hermione Granger in the Harry Potter movies, British actress Emma Watson is a real heroine offscreen. In 2014, she became a Global Goodwill Ambassador for UN Women, the United Nations organization dedicated to gender equality and the empowerment of women. Soon after, Watson made a game-changing speech at United Nations Headquarters, in which she said that feminism isn't just a women's issue—it's a human rights issue. For the movement to have any chance of success, she said, men need to stand up and speak out for gender equality. So far, at least one man in every single country in the world—including world leaders and global CEOs—has joined HeForShe, a UN Women's uniting movement for gender equality.

Political Caucus, aimed at getting more women to participate in politics. That same year, she founded a feminist magazine called *Ms.* Everyone had their doubts. Even Steinem thought *Ms.* would never be anything more than a single sample magazine—which was all its founders could get a publisher to agree to produce. But its 300,000 test copies sold out in eight days, and *Ms.* is still in print today. Nearly 50 years later, Steinem pens best-selling books and travels the world to spread her message: that women can do anything men can do.

FROM BOXES TO

There's nothing like a trip to the ocean: the soft sand, the cool water, the ... corset pinching your rib cage? In the early 1800s, people began to flock to the beach to splash in the surf. But it was a time when women barely showed their ankles beyond the privacy of their own homes. How could one possibly swim and stay modest? Some of the solutions might surprise you—or make you laugh. Either way, it took a true heroine to sport this swimwear!

Bikinis

FROM HIGH-NECKED COLLARS TO HIGH-PERFORMANCE SWIMSUITS

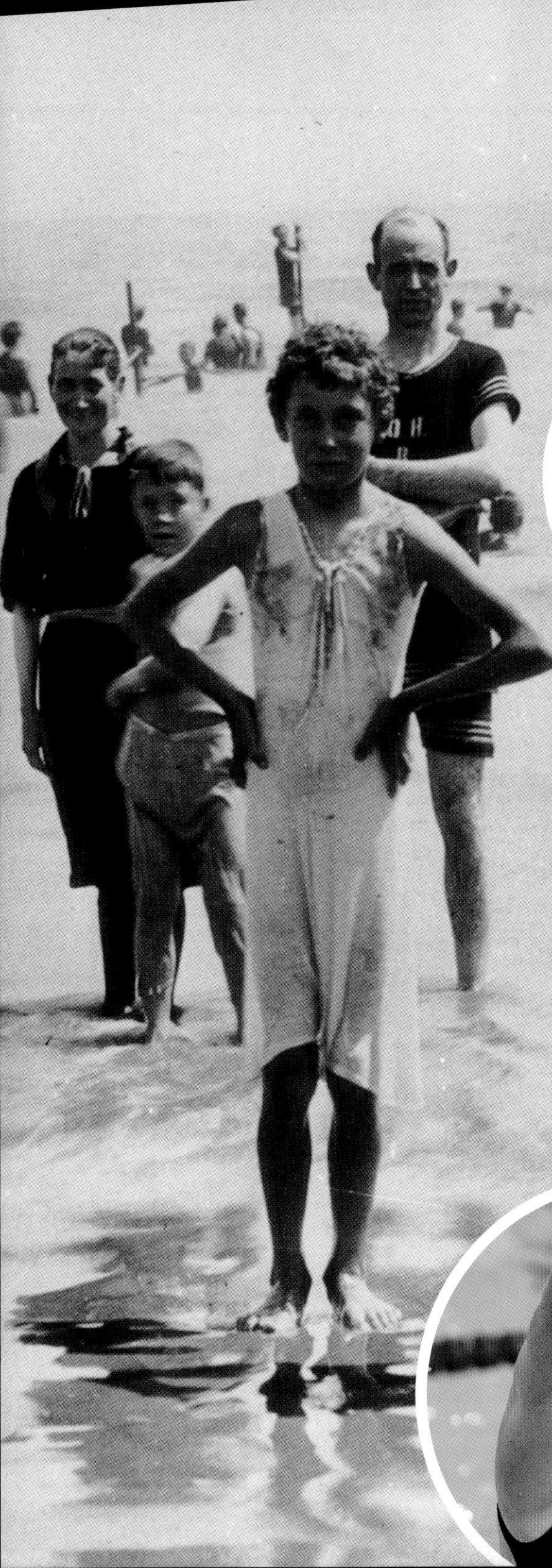

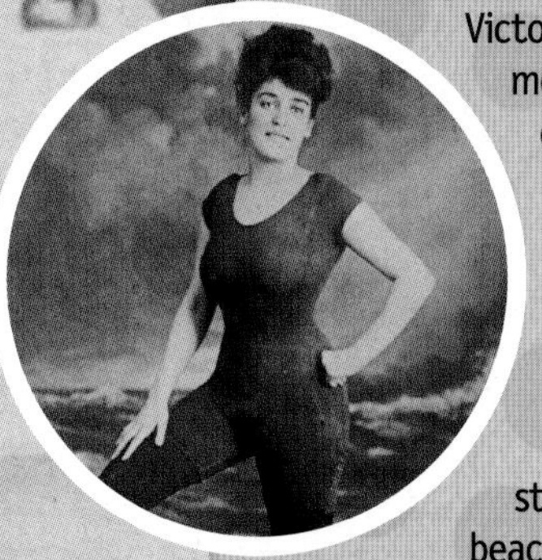

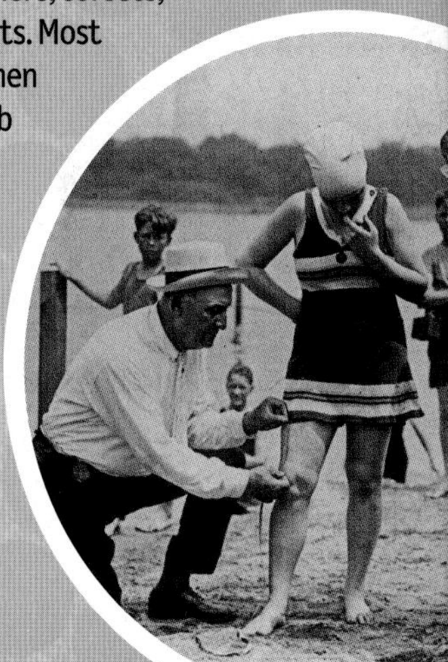

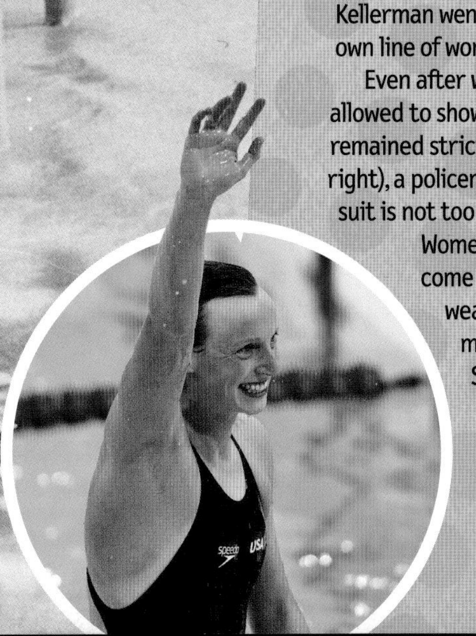

Around the 1750s, before swimwear was invented, strange, wheeled boxes began popping up on beaches. They were bathing machines, an extreme way to protect Victorian ladies' tender modesty. The brave swimmer would enter the box, which was then carted out to sea so she could take a dip far from prying eyes.

When women were allowed to actually swim in public, they might not have wanted to. Early bathing suits were made of approximately four yards (3.7 m) of heavy wool, with skirts over bloomers, corsets, stockings, shoes, and hats. Most beaches had ropes for women to hold on to so their heavy garb didn't drag them underwater.

Competitive swimmer Annette Kellerman, sick of her wool skirts keeping her from enjoying the ocean, hit a Boston beach in 1907 wearing a one-piece swimsuit (above). She was arrested. In court, she complained, "I may as well be swimming in chains." Kellerman went on to develop her own line of women's swimwear.

Even after women were finally allowed to show their legs, the rules remained strict. In this photo from 1925 (above right), a policeman measures to make sure a bather's suit is not too far north of her knee.

Women's swimwear—and women's rights—have come a long way. Today, competitive swimmers wear sleek, aerodynamic suits that help them move through the water as quickly as possible. Shown at left in a swimsuit fit for competition, rising superstar Katie Ledecky wins gold in the 800-meter freestyle at the 2012 London Olympics. Read more about Ledecky on page 36.

Malala YOUSAFZAI

SHE REFUSES TO BE AFRAID

History books are full of people who showed courage in the face of danger, but most of them were much older than 15-year-old Malala Yousafzai. This fearless girl spoke out for justice—and it almost cost her everything.

PATH TO FREEDOM

When class let out on October 9, 2012, Malala walked out of school and got on the bus, just as she normally did. As she chatted with her friend Moniba, Malala noticed that the road—usually busy—seemed unusually quiet. Suddenly, two strange men flagged down the bus. As they boarded, Moniba heard one of them say, "Who is Malala?" He then pointed a pistol at Malala and fired.

The attacker shot Malala in the head. The bullet struck above her left eyebrow and traveled down her neck. Two of her friends were also injured by the gunfire. Malala was flown to Queen Elizabeth Hospital in the United Kingdom, where a doctor performed emergency surgery to save her life.

> "THEY WANTED TO SILENCE ONE MALALA, BUT INSTEAD NOW THOUSANDS AND MILLIONS OF MALALAS ARE SPEAKING."
> —MALALA YOUSAFZAI

FEARLESS FACTS

→ **BORN:** July 12, 1997, Mingora, Pakistan → **STUDENT ACTIVIST:** Student and activist
→ **BOLDEST MOMENT:** Risking death to stand up for justice

SPEAKING OUT

The gunman who shot Malala was trying to silence her. When she was 11, members of a militant group called the Taliban controlled Pakistan's Swat Valley, where Malala lived. They ruled by fear, banning television, books, and education for women. Between 2007 and 2011, the Taliban destroyed more than 400 schools in the Swat Valley.

Before her shooting, Malala had been blogging for the BBC, a news organization, about what was happening in her town. She chronicled what life was like under Taliban rule. She wrote about how she wanted to return to school and become a doctor. She said that she was afraid of the Taliban but that she was determined not to let fear stop her from getting an education. At first, she wrote without revealing her name. But then, after she appeared in a documentary by the *New York Times*, Taliban leaders learned who she was—and they decided to kill her. The Taliban later said that when they shot Malala they were trying to teach a lesson to those who dared to stand up for freedom and education.

A BRIGHTER FUTURE

Malala nearly died from her injuries. Today, she has a titanium plate in her head and an implant that helps her hear because the bullet left her deaf in one ear. But the attack made Malala famous, as she became a symbol for children around the world who are denied an education. In 2014, Malala became the youngest person in history to win the Nobel Peace Prize, one of the highest honors in the world.

Today, the Malala Fund raises money to bring education to girls who need it most. On July 12, 2015, Malala celebrated her 18th birthday by opening a school for girls in Lebanon. She has proven that one person—even if they're just a kid—can make a world of difference.

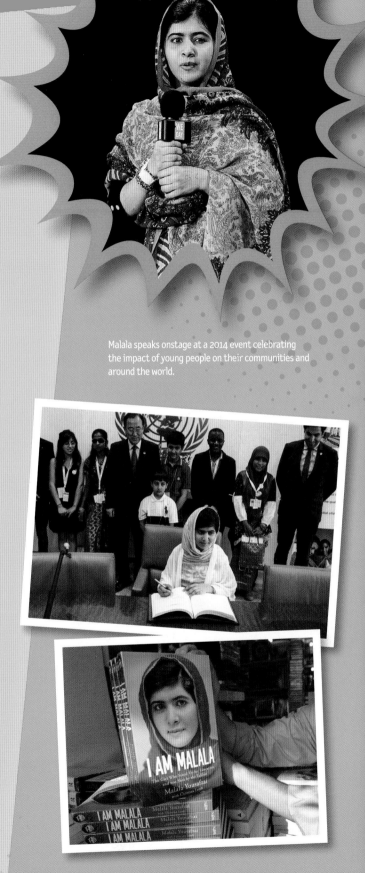

Malala speaks onstage at a 2014 event celebrating the impact of young people on their communities and around the world.

Malala at the United Nations in 2013 (middle), and her best-selling book, published the same year (bottom)

JUSTICE SEEKERS
HUMAN RIGHTS HEROINES

When these women witnessed injustice in the world around them, they didn't just sit back and let it happen. They became the voices of those who didn't have the power to speak for themselves—from African Americans to migrant workers to the disabled. Their actions helped bring justice to those who needed it most.

TIRELESS ADVOCATE: Helen Keller (1880–1968)

When Helen Keller was two years old, she became very sick with what modern doctors now think was scarlet fever or meningitis. She survived, but the illness took her vision, hearing, and ability to speak. The frustrated, lonely Helen grew wild and unruly. Many of her relatives thought she should be put away in an institution. Then, when Helen was seven, her parents hired teacher Anne Sullivan, who taught Helen sign language and gave her a way to communicate with the world for the first time.

Helen's newfound ability empowered her. She graduated from Radcliffe College in 1904, becoming the first deaf and blind person to earn a bachelor of arts degree. She learned to speak, and she became a world-famous lecturer and author who advocated for people with disabilities. She also tackled many social issues, including workers' rights and women's suffrage. She helped found the American Civil Liberties Union (ACLU), which works to support individuals' rights and liberties. Today, Keller is a symbol for how courage and hard work can triumph over adversity.

UNSTOPPABLE: Shirley Chisholm (1924–2005)

In 1949, Shirley Chisholm joined the Democratic Party club in her Brooklyn, New York, U.S.A., neighborhood, where two-thirds of the community was black but were represented by white politicians. When she questioned the party leadership and pushed them to recognize the issues of black voters, they tried to quiet her by giving her an important title as a member of the board of directors. When Chisholm still refused to go along with their actions, they kicked her out. It was the beginning of a career Chisholm would spend questioning those in power. She entered politics, campaigning for the rights of women and minorities. Her outspoken approach won her respect. In 1968, she became the first black woman elected to Congress, and in 1972, she even ran for president—the first African-American woman in history to do so.

BRING U.S. TOGETHER

VOTE CHISHOLM 1972
UNBOUGHT AND UNBOSSED

ORGANIZING PROGRESS: Dolores Huerta (1930–)

At the elementary school where Dolores Huerta taught in Stockton, California, U.S.A., students were mostly the children of farmworkers who labored under terrible conditions. They didn't have cold drinking water or restrooms in the fields, and they made very little money. Huerta's students often came to school hungry and without shoes. Resolving that the best way to help her students was to help their parents, in 1960 Huerta created the Agricultural Workers Association, which lobbied politicians for greater rights for migrant workers. In 1962, she and activist Cesar Chavez co-founded United Farm Workers, a union that encouraged farm workers to organize so they could demand more money and rights. In her lifetime, Huerta has helped bring national attention and greater quality to the lives of workers, immigrants, and women.

STANDING HER GROUND: Aung San Suu Kyi (1945–)

When a young Aung San Suu Kyi returned to her home country of Myanmar in 1988 after years of living abroad, she was shocked by what she saw. Myanmar was ruled by a brutal dictator named U Ne Win who slaughtered any protesters who dared oppose him. At great personal danger, Kyi began speaking out publicly against him. In 1989, his military government put her under house arrest. The military told Kyi that she would be freed if she agreed to leave the country, but she refused to go until peace was restored to Myanmar. She spent 15 of the next 21 years in custody. Today, Kyi is an international symbol of peaceful resistance.

UNDETERRED BY DANGER: Asma Jahangir (1952–)

Asma Jahangir launched her first legal fight at age 20, when she battled to free her father, who had spent years in prison and under house arrest for opposing Pakistan's military dictatorships. She went on to earn a law degree and to found the first all-female law firm in Pakistan to defend the rights of women there. In 1986, Jahangir created the Human Rights Commission of Pakistan, which combats the many human rights injustices committed in her country. These include abuse toward women, death sentences given to protesters, and the illegal torture of prisoners. Jahangir has been threatened, attacked, and placed under house arrest, but she has never stopped helping the people who need her.

123

Anne FRANK

THE VOICE OF HOPE

On her 13th birthday, Anne Frank's family gave her a red-checkered diary. Like the average teenage girl, Anne wrote about her relationship with her parents and her crushes on boys. But she also wrote about horrors that most teenagers can't imagine experiencing. Two years earlier, the Nazis had taken over Amsterdam, Holland, where Anne lived, and they were sending Jews to concentration camps by the thousands. The Frank family lived in fear that they would be next.

In 1942, the Frank family, along with four other Dutch Jews, went into hiding in a small series of makeshift rooms in an empty space behind Anne's father's office. For two years, Dutch friends smuggled them food and information. All the while, Anne faithfully recorded her hopes and fears in her diary.

On August 4, 1944, the Nazis discovered the hiding place and sent everyone there to concentration camps. In March 1945, at Bergen-Belsen concentration camp in northern Germany, Anne died of typhus at the age of 15. She was one of more than a million Jewish children who died in the Holocaust. All together, six million Jews lost their lives—more than half the Jewish population of Europe.

Though Anne didn't survive World War II, her diary did. When her father discovered it after the war, he was so amazed by Anne's account of her time in hiding that he had it published. *The Diary of a Young Girl* is still one of the most famous books in the world. Though Anne's story is a tragedy, her diary is an account of love in the face of hate. "I feel the suffering of millions," she wrote. "And yet, when I look up at the sky, I somehow feel that everything will change for the better, that this cruelty too shall end, that peace and tranquility will return once more."

> "I STILL BELIEVE, IN SPITE OF EVERYTHING, THAT PEOPLE ARE TRULY GOOD AT HEART."
> —ANNE FRANK

FEARLESS FACTS

BORN: June 12, 1929, Frankfurt, Germany **DIED:** March 1945, Bergen-Belsen concentration camp, Lower Saxony, Germany **OCCUPATION:** Writer **BOLDEST MOMENT:** Telling a story that has inspired generations

Sophie SCHOLL

THE FACE OF RESISTANCE

> "WHAT WE WROTE AND SAID IS ALSO BELIEVED BY MANY OTHERS. THEY JUST DON'T DARE TO EXPRESS THEMSELVES AS WE DID."
> —SOPHIE SCHOLL

Like many other Germans in the late 1930s, Sophie Scholl and her brother Hans listened to Adolf Hitler's speeches and were persuaded he was leading their country to greatness. But the Scholls' wise father, Robert, warned his children that Hitler was actually leading Germany toward destruction. In time, the siblings came to realize that their father was right.

Sophie and Hans and their group of friends felt it was their duty to stand up to the evil regime that was sending hundreds of thousands of citizens to their deaths. They formed a small resistance group and called it the White Rose. In 1942, they wrote an essay asserting that the Nazi system was destroying the German people and that it was time for Germans to rise up in protest. They secretly distributed copies around the University of Munich. They penned more essays and began mailing thousands of copies to locations all over Germany and Austria.

The Nazi police (or Gestapo) were desperate to catch the White Rose. The resistance group was careful, but their luck finally ran out on February 18, 1943. A custodian saw Hans and Sophie leaving pamphlets at the University of Munich and reported them to the police. Sophie and the other members of the White Rose didn't try to hide what they had done. They stood up for the morality of their actions, despite the dire consequences it could bring. Sophie, Hans, and a friend were deemed guilty of treason and sentenced to death, but the story of their bravery and humanity in the face of evil endures.

FEARLESS FACTS

➲ **BORN:** May 9, 1921, Forchtenberg, Germany ➲ **DIED:** February 22, 1943, Stadelheim Prison, Munich, Germany ➲ **OCCUPATION:** Student, activist ➲ **BOLDEST MOMENT:** Standing up for her beliefs and against the Nazi regime

MOMENT OF BRAVERY

Heroines come in all sizes. This six-year-old wasn't too little to make a big impression. How did her considerable courage change society?

THE SITUATION

The year was 1960. In Ruby Bridges's home of New Orleans, Louisiana, U.S.A., schools were segregated, with African-American children and white children separated. Little Ruby lived just five blocks from an all-white school, but every day she had to travel several miles to attend kindergarten at her all-black school.

Then, a court ordered that New Orleans' schools must integrate. Ruby and her schoolmates had to take a test that determined which black students would go to white schools. It was rumored that officials opposed to the new ruling designed the test to be so difficult that students would have trouble passing—but Ruby did. Ruby learned that she would be the first black child to attend an all-white elementary school in the South.

THE MOMENT OF TRUTH

On the morning of November 14, 1960, police officers drove Ruby and her mother the five blocks to school. When they got to the building, there was an angry mob waiting for them outside. People chanted, "Two-four-six-eight, we don't want to integrate." To get an education, the first grader would have to walk right through the furious crowd.

Wearing a pink dress and clutching her schoolbag and lunch box, six-year-old Ruby stood up tall and marched into the school. A photograph of the little girl surrounded by policemen protecting her from angry protesters is one of the most famous pictures of the civil rights movement.

THE LEGACY

Many white parents of students at Ruby's school were so upset that Ruby had been allowed to join that they pulled their children out of class. Some of them even threatened to hurt Ruby. Ruby's dad lost his job, and her grandparents lost their tenant farm. No parents would let their children be in the same classroom as Ruby—or even on the same floor. Every day for a year, a teacher named Mrs. Henry taught Ruby alone. Ruby couldn't eat in the cafeteria or go to recess, so she spent all day, every day in Mrs. Henry's classroom. Today, the two women (left) are still friends. Ruby was lonely, but she never missed a day of class. When she started second grade the next year, Ruby walked into a classroom full of both white and African-American kids. History was changed forever, and it couldn't have happened without her.

CHAPTER SEVEN

Ladies in LAB COATS

The word "heroine" probably doesn't make you think of Bunsen burners and protective goggles. But consider this: Without achievements in science, we wouldn't have bulletproof vests, computer programming, or nuclear power. Oh, and all those discoveries? Women made them—no easy feat in fields dominated by men. Even today, women hold only about a quarter of science jobs, and for female scientists of the past, the going was even tougher. But that didn't stop these brainy ladies from rolling up their sleeves and changing the world.

Nobel Prize–winner Marie Curie
works in her laboratory.

Marie CURIE

SHE GAVE HER LIFE TO SCIENCE

On February 26, 1896, a French physicist named Henri Becquerel absentmindedly tossed a bit of uranium in a drawer, on top of an undeveloped photographic plate—a light-sensitive sheet used to capture images before the invention of film. When Becquerel returned later, he was surprised to find that there was a mark on the plate where the uranium had been. It looked just like the plate had been exposed to light—but it hadn't. The only explanation was that the uranium must be emitting some sort of mysterious rays.

Becquerel turned the discovery over to a young graduate student. Her name was Marie Curie. She would go on to become the most famous woman in the history of science. But it was her dedication to the subject that would also eventually lead to her death.

FOR THE LOVE OF SCIENCE

Young Maria "Marie" Sklodowska was a top student who loved math and science but who—because she was a woman—was banned from attending the University of Warsaw in her Polish hometown. So Marie set her sights on the Sorbonne, a school in Paris, France, graduating first in her class with a degree in physics in 1893.

The following year, Marie began sharing lab space with another scientist: Pierre Curie. Marie and Pierre may have been physicists, but these two had chemistry.

> "BE LESS CURIOUS ABOUT PEOPLE AND MORE CURIOUS ABOUT IDEAS."
> —MARIE CURIE

FEARLESS FACTS

➥ **BORN:** November 7, 1867, Warsaw, Poland ➥ **DIED:** July 4, 1934, Passy, France
➥ **OCCUPATION:** Physicist ➥ **BOLDEST MOMENT:** Discovering radioactivity

They fell in love, got married, and became science's power couple. They would work side by side for 20 years, until Pierre was tragically killed by a horse-drawn carriage in 1906.

After she graduated, Curie turned her impressive intellect to the mystery of Becquerel's uranium. She figured out that its peculiar rays were actually a new type of extremely powerful energy, emitted from the very structure of the uranium atoms themselves. She dubbed this energy "radioactivity." Her findings the following year shed light on the inner workings of atoms and revolutionized the fields of physics and chemistry.

IT'S ELEMENTARY

Pierre was so fascinated with Marie's work that he quit his research to help his wife. The pair worked to find the sources of the energy in chunks of radioactive rock. In 1898, they found one: a new radioactive element unknown to science. They named it polonium, after Marie's native country of Poland. In 1902, they discovered another: radium. To test the elements, the Curies had to extract them from rocks, which was tough work. Marie often stayed up late stirring huge cauldrons with an iron rod nearly as tall as she was.

Curie's hard work paid off. In 1903, she made history when she became the first woman to receive the Nobel Prize. She won for her work on radioactivity, along with her husband and Henri Becquerel. In 1911, after Pierre's death, Marie won a second Nobel Prize for her discovery of polonium and radium. That made her the first person in history—male or female—to win two Nobel Prizes. But her breakthroughs came at a terrible cost. In 1934, at age 66, she died of leukemia, a blood cancer most likely caused by a lifetime of working with radioactive materials. Curie left a legacy that made it clear a woman could be a great scientist. She inspired a new generation of female scientists—including a daughter named Irène Joliot-Curie who won the Nobel Prize in 1935.

Pierre and Marie Curie in 1898 (above); equipment used by the Curies to investigate the electrical conductivity of air exposed to radium (right)

DANGEROUS DISCOVERY: RADIATION

Modern scientists use lead shields and remote sensors to study radioactive materials from a safe distance. That's because if living cells are exposed to radiation, they can become cancerous. But Marie Curie had no idea her new discovery was unsafe—she carried radioactive rocks around in her pocket! In fact, for a long time, people thought that something so incredibly energetic as radiation must be healthy. Manufacturers put radioactive thorium in toothpaste and laxatives. Visitors to the Glen Springs Hotel in the Finger Lakes region of New York, U.S.A., could take a dip in its radioactive mineral springs. It wasn't until 1938 that radioactivity was banned from consumer products. Even now, Curie's papers from the 1890s are too dangerous to handle.

INSPIRING INVENTORS
EXTRAORDINARY EVERYDAY PRODUCTS

Imagine a driver navigating a rainy highway without windshield wipers, or a police officer facing down an armed criminal without protective body armor. It's hard to believe there was a time before these inventions existed! Ready for one more mind-boggler? Both of these products—and many others—were invented by women!

WINDSHIELD WIPERS: Mary Anderson (1866–1953)

On a snowy day in 1903, Mary Anderson was squinting out the window of a New York City trolley car, trying to see the sights through blowing snow. She had traveled all the way from Birmingham, Alabama, U.S.A., to take in the Big Apple's tall buildings and bustling streets, but the weather was ruining her plans. It wasn't helping the trolley driver, either: Anderson noticed that every few minutes, he had to stop and reach through his window to brush snow off his windshield by hand. That gave her an idea. She filed a patent for the first windshield wiper: a rubber blade that would drag across the windshield when the driver pulled a lever near his steering wheel. At first, companies were afraid Anderson's invention would just distract drivers. But by 1916, her creation was standard on most vehicles.

KEVLAR: Stephanie Kwolek (1923–2014)

As a kid, Stephanie Kwolek loved fabric and sewing. But instead of becoming a fashion designer, she became one of the world's first female research chemists. While working at the DuPont chemical company, she was assigned to develop a strong, lightweight fiber to be used in car tires. One day, she put a liquid she had created into a spinning machine, and the molecules in the liquid lined up in long chains, creating a fiber. That fiber became Kevlar: a material that's lightweight, fireproof, and five times as strong as steel. Today, Kevlar is used to make countless products, from kayaks to spacecraft to—most famously—bulletproof body armor. Since police officers started using Kevlar body armor in 1975, Kwolek's invention has saved about 3,000 lives.

LIQUID PAPER: Bette Nesmith Graham (1922–1980)

In 1951, single mom Bette Nesmith Graham started working as a secretary to support her son. Unlike today's personal computers, which come with a handy delete key, making a typo while using a typewriter back then meant you had to start all over. Not wanting to waste time, Graham began using white paint to cover up her errors, then typed over them. Her boss never noticed, but the other secretaries in the office did. They asked Graham to share her secret, so she started bottling her product—which she named Mistake Out—and passed it around. In 1956, she turned her kitchen into a laboratory, concocting a new formula with her kitchen mixer. After making a mistake at work too big for white paint to fix, Graham got fired—but she took her unexpected unemployment as an opportunity and threw herself full-time into her new company, now called Liquid Paper. By 1976, she had a factory making 500 bottles a minute.

CHOCOLATE CHIP COOKIES: Ruth Wakefield (1903–1977)

Ruth Wakefield and her husband owned a lodge in Whitman, Massachusetts, U.S.A., called the Toll House Inn. Wakefield whipped up all the food for their guests and had a reputation as a brilliant baker. So she didn't panic when, one day in 1930, she realized she was out of the baker's chocolate she needed for a batch of cookies she was mixing up. Instead, she reached for the closest substitute: a semisweet chocolate bar. Wakefield chopped up the bar, tossed the chunks in the dough, and crossed her fingers. When she pulled the cookies out of the oven, she discovered that, unlike baker's chocolate, the chocolate bar chunks didn't melt to create chocolate-flavored batter. Instead, the pieces softened into delicious gooey morsels. Wakefield had improvised her way into an iconic American dessert: the chocolate chip cookie. Nestle started printing her recipe on its bags of chocolate chips. It's still the most popular back-of-the-package recipe today.

WEB WONDER: DARING DUDE Timothy Berners-Lee (1955–)

No single inventor can claim credit for the Internet, which dates back to the early 1960s when computer scientists began brainstorming a system for researchers, educators, and government agencies to share information through their computers. But English computer scientist Timothy Berners-Lee helped turn the Internet into a tool for everybody. In 1989, he invented hypertext transfer protocol (HTTP), a language of rules that lets computers share information over the Internet through a system of linked pages that Berners-Lee called the World Wide Web. Berners-Lee's system blossomed into an essential worldwide resource for information, communication, and cute kitty videos.

Sara SEAGER

PLANET HUNTER

When you look at the stars dotting the night sky, do you ever wonder if somewhere out there, another being is gazing back at you? It sounds like sci-fi, but alien life might not be as unlikely as you think.

Scientists estimate that there are more than 100 billion galaxies in the universe, each one of them home to tens of billions of stars. Orbiting many of these are planets that have the right conditions for life. One group of experts estimates that the universe holds about five trillion of these habitable worlds. (To get an idea of how many that is, consider this: five trillion seconds is more than 150,000 years.) In short: The universe is so big that, odds are, we're not alone. And Sara Seager is 100 percent confident that it's only a matter of time before we find out who we share it with.

While studying astrophysics at Harvard University, Seager became one of the first people to research exoplanets—faraway worlds scientists were beginning to find with powerful new telescopes. She came up with a novel way of studying the atmosphere, or layers of gases, that surrounds these faraway planets: By looking at the color of an exoplanet, she can tell what its atmosphere is made of. Seager is on the hunt for planets whose atmospheres contain gases—like oxygen, ozone, and methane—known to be produced by living organisms. If she detects them, she's hit the jackpot—a planet that could harbor alien life. Seager predicts that will happen within 20 years.

> "BEING A SCIENTIST IS LIKE BEING AN EXPLORER."
> —SARA SEAGER

FEARLESS FACTS

➔ **BORN:** July 21, 1971, Toronto, Canada ➔ **OCCUPATION:** Astrophysicist
➔ **BOLDEST MOMENT:** Predicting the discovery of alien life within 20 years

Jennifer DOUDNA

GENETICS GAME CHANGER

Genes are bits of inherited information that control how a living thing looks or acts. Would you believe that humans have actually been modifying genes for thousands of years? It's true: By deciding which organisms to breed, we've created dogs with flat faces; corn with sweet, juicy kernels; and all sorts of other living things with traits that appeal to us.

In recent decades, scientists have even figured out how to directly delete or replace specific genes using genetic engineering, but the technology has been expensive and hard to use. That changed in 2012, when a biochemist named Jennifer Doudna led a team that discovered a way to hack a molecule found in ancient bacteria and turn it into a tool for editing genes. Using a DNA "address," scientists can send the molecule, called CRISPR, to a specific location in a strand of DNA. Once there, it follows their instructions to cut out or add in a new gene as easily as you can use a computer to edit a sentence.

CRISPR's potential is huge. Researchers could use the simple, inexpensive technology to eliminate genetic diseases like muscular dystrophy, stop cancer cells from growing, and end world hunger by creating crops that can grow in any climate. Nearly every genetics lab in the world is already starting to experiment with CRISPR. But with the technology's great power comes great responsibility, so experts are currently working together to create rules for using CRISPR responsibly. One thing they agree on: Doudna's discovery is going to change science in a big way.

> "I REALLY WANT TO SEE THIS TECHNOLOGY USED TO HELP PEOPLE."
> —JENNIFER DOUDNA

FEARLESS FACTS

- **BORN:** February 19, 1964, Washington, D.C.
- **OCCUPATION:** Biochemist
- **BOLDEST MOMENT:** Making DNA editing almost effortless

BRAINY LADIES
MAKING THE UNKNOWN KNOWN

These bold women weren't afraid to venture all over the universe in the name of science, from the bottom of the sea to the farthest reaches of the galaxy—and even back in time! Their valiant efforts were rewarded: These brainy ladies are responsible for some of science's most incredible finds.

LADY OF LIGHT:
Lene Vestergaard Hau (1959–)

It's not easy to control the fastest thing in the universe: light. So Lene Vestergaard Hau's work makes her the closest thing there is to a real-life magician. Normally, light zips around at 186,282 miles per second (299,792 km/sec). But Hau discovered that by shooting pulses of laser light through a cloud of super-cold sodium atoms, she could slow light down. In 2001, she was able to make a pulse of light stop completely! She could soon control light at will, making it stop, start, and even disappear and reappear in a completely different place. When asked what Einstein—who set light's speed limit—would have thought of her work, Hau said modestly, "I'm sure he would have been rather surprised."

HER DEEPNESS: Sylvia Earle (1935–)

When Sylvia Earle was in graduate school studying marine biology, she applied for a position as a teaching assistant. Even though she was the best qualified applicant, she didn't get the job. "They said, 'It has to go to a man, because a woman will just get married and have babies,'" she remembers. They probably regret passing her over now. For the past five decades, Earle—who has won countless awards for her work and earned the nickname Her Deepness—has clocked more than 7,000

MISTRESS OF MATTER: Vera Rubin (1928–)

When Vera Rubin was 14, she turned a cardboard tube into a home-made telescope and started scanning the sky. She never stopped. Once she'd earned a degree in astronomy, she started watching stars out near the edges of galaxies and noticed something she didn't expect to see: These stars were spinning very fast. That was odd, because the galaxy holding them wasn't big enough to keep the twirling stars in orbit. Rubin realized that there must be something else out there holding them in place—something really massive. It was the first evidence of the existence of what scientists call dark matter. Scientists still don't know how to detect dark matter—or even what it is—but they estimate that it makes up about 27 percent of the universe.

TIME TRAVELER:
Adriana C. Ocampo (1955–)

Adriana Ocampo's work takes her far into the past. But to get there, she doesn't use a time machine: Ocampo is a planetary geologist who examines rocks to learn about a planet's history. She started working for NASA at a summer job in 1973, when she was still a teenager, and has since worked on missions to map planets, including Pluto and Jupiter. In 1989, Ocampo was studying satellite images of Mexico's coastline when she spotted something no one had noticed before: a gargantuan crater buried beneath the Yucatán Peninsula. It turned out to be a 130-mile (209-km)-wide scar left over from when a huge asteroid slammed into Earth 65 million years ago, wiping out about half of the world's plants and animals—including the dinosaurs.

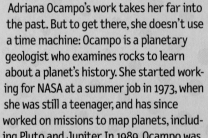

hours exploring the deep oceans. She's discovered thousands of species, led more than 50 expeditions, and set a record for the lowest depth a human has explored on foot when she took a stroll 1,250 feet (381 m) below the surface of the Pacific Ocean. In 2009, she started a foundation called Mission Blue, which aims to create protected areas of the ocean—similar to what national parks do on land.

"We need many things to keep and maintain the world as a better place," Earle has said. "But nothing else will matter if we fail to protect the ocean."

Snubbed by SCIENCE

These female scientists got the short end of the stick. Each one made an amazing discovery...and was then sidelined as a male scientist got the credit instead. But here we're pulling them off the periphery and onto the trophy stand. We salute you, unsung heroines of science!

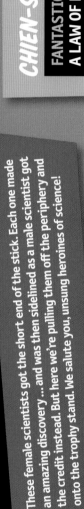

DID SHE EVER GET CREDIT? NO

CHIEN-SHIUNG WU (1912–1997)

FANTASTIC FEAT: SHE OVERTURNED A LAW OF PHYSICS.

For many years, physicists believed in something called the Parity Law, which stated that objects that are mirror images of each other must behave in the same way. Wu proved this wasn't true by spinning the nuclei of radioactive cobalt-60 atoms. If the Parity Law was correct, the cobalt's electrons should shoot off in pairs—but they didn't. Her work was called "the solution to the number one riddle of atomic and nuclear physics." Her male colleagues at Columbia University in New York City won a Nobel Prize for the discovery, while Wu was overlooked.

DID SHE EVER GET CREDIT? NOT UNTIL HER CONTRIBUTIONS TO COMPUTER SCIENCE WERE DISCOVERED IN THE 1950s.

ADA LOVELACE (1815–1852)

FANTASTIC FEAT: SHE WAS THE WORLD'S FIRST COMPUTER PROGRAMMER.

When she was 18, Ada Lovelace met Charles Babbage, a mathematician famous for making elaborate, unfinished plans for enormous calculating machines. United by a love of math and logic, Lovelace and Babbage became good friends. In 1842, Babbage asked Lovelace to translate an article about one of his machines from Italian into English. Lovelace did one better, adding her own notes describing how codes could make the device able to handle not just numbers, but letters and symbols as well. Today, she's recognized as the first computer programmer.

DID SHE EVER GET CREDIT? NO

ROSALIND FRANKLIN (1920–1958)

FANTASTIC FEAT: SHE WAS KEY TO DISCOVERING THE STRUCTURE OF DNA.

Rosalind Franklin was a chemist who used x-rays to take detailed photographs of DNA, the molecule that stores the genetic information of all living things. Other scientists—James Watson and Francis Crick—used one of her photographs to create a model of DNA's structure. Watson and Crick won a Nobel Prize and didn't credit Franklin for her role in the discovery.

JOCELYN BELL BURNELL (1943–)

FANTASTIC FEAT: SHE DISCOVERED A NEW TYPE OF STAR.

Astrophysicist Jocelyn Bell Burnell was in charge of analyzing charts of data from a radio telescope aimed at the stars. There was a lot to look at—the data covered more than three miles (4.8 km) of paper! But Burnell stuck with it. After several weeks, she noticed strange markings in some of the charts. She had detected the first known pulsar: an incredibly dense star left over from a giant star that had exploded in a supernova. The finding resulted in a Nobel Prize—for Burnell's male supervisor and another male astronomer.

DID SHE EVER GET CREDIT? NO

DID SHE EVER GET CREDIT?
NOT UNTIL YEARS LATER, WHEN HER OBSERVATIONS WERE CONFIRMED BY A MAN.

CECILIA PAYNE-GAPOSCHKIN (1900–1979)

FANTASTIC FEAT: SHE DISCOVERED THE INGREDIENTS OF STARS.

She set out to answer one of the most important questions of astrophysics: What are stars made of? By studying the colors in the light emitted by stars, she was able to figure out what elements form them: Stars are formed almost entirely of hydrogen and helium, with the other 116 elements making up less than 2 percent of them. Astronomer Otto Struve would later call Payne-Gaposchkin's 1925 paper explaining her findings "the most brilliant... ever written in astronomy." But at the time, her colleagues dismissed her observations—until a male colleague confirmed them four years later.

HENRIETTA LACKS (1920–1951)

FANTASTIC FEAT: HER CELLS HAVE BEEN USED EXTENSIVELY FOR MEDICAL RESEARCH.

Henrietta Lacks was a tobacco farmer from Virginia, U.S.A., who had a cancerous tumor removed when she was 30 years old. While she was undergoing surgery, doctors took cells from her tumor and gave them to other scientists to study—without asking Lacks for her permission. Those scientists found something surprising: Unlike other human cells, which only lived for a few days in the lab, Lacks's cells stayed alive and grew. Her cells have since been used in the polio vaccine, chemotherapy, cloning, and many other groundbreaking medical advancements. The cells even blasted off in the first space missions so scientists could find out what happens to cells in zero gravity. Henrietta never knew her cells were taken.

DID SHE EVER GET CREDIT?
NOT UNTIL 2010, WHEN AUTHOR REBECCA SKLOOT WROTE A BEST-SELLING BOOK ABOUT LACKS. SINCE THEN, SHE'S BEEN HONORED BY THE SMITHSONIAN INSTITUTION AND THE NATIONAL FOUNDATION FOR CANCER RESEARCH AND AWARDED AN HONORARY DEGREE BY MORGAN STATE UNIVERSITY.

Rachel CARSON

PROTECTOR OF THE PLANET

"THOSE WHO DWELL ... AMONG THE BEAUTIES AND MYSTERIES OF THE EARTH ARE NEVER ALONE OR WEARY OF LIFE."
—RACHEL CARSON

In 1939, Swiss chemist Paul Müller discovered the world's first man-made pesticide: DDT (short for dichlorodiphenyltrichloroethane). It was inexpensive, easy to use, and extremely effective at killing pesky pests. Farmers who sprayed it on their fields harvested a bounty of fruit and vegetables. It brought insect-spread diseases like malaria under control. The world hailed DDT as a miracle product.

What nobody knew then was that DDT is highly toxic. With the world unaware, DDT began building up in the tissues of Earth's living things. But there was one voice that spoke out against the dangers of DDT. It belonged to Rachel Carson, and it forever changed the way humans see the world around them.

FROM LAB TO LIBRARY

After she graduated from college, Rachel got a job working for the U.S. Fish and Wildlife Service as a marine biologist. On the side, she wrote articles for magazines teaching people about the ocean. In 1951, she wrote a book called *The Sea Around Us*, which was on the *New York Times* Best Sellers List for 80 weeks. With her book's success, Rachel was able to quit her job and write full time.

Carson had grown worried about the possible

FEARLESS FACTS

➲ **BORN:** May 27, 1907, Springdale, Pennsylvania, U.S.A. ➲ **DIED:** April 14, 1964, Silver Spring, Maryland, U.S.A. w **OCCUPATION:** Marine biologist, writer ➲ **BOLDEST MOMENT:** Starting the environmental revolution

dangers of pesticides while working for the U.S. Fish and Wildlife Service. Scientists there had found some warning signs that DDT was harmful to fish and other ocean life. When companies started selling DDT, in 1945, Carson's concern grew. She hoped that someone would write an article warning people about the dangers of DDT—but no one did.

Then, in 1957, Carson got a letter from an old friend in Massachusetts, U.S.A., saying that birds there were mysteriously dying. Carson worried that DDT—which was sprayed in the air as pest control—might be the secret avian assassin. The terrible possibility that someday spring might come without birdsong convinced Carson that the world needed to know about the dangers of pesticides.

SILENT SPRING

Carson spent four years tirelessly researching her subject. She interviewed scientists who studied pesticides, including DDT. The experts explained that DDT grows more dangerous as it moves up the food chain. For example, if the water in a lake contains small amounts of DDT, the fish that live in that water will have small amounts of the pesticide in their bodies. Seabirds have to eat a lot of fish to survive, so, over time, DDT builds up in their tissues. Animals near the top of the food chain—such as the falcons that dine on seabirds—have more DDT in them still.

In 1962, Carson published her famous book *Silent Spring*, which claimed that DDT and other pesticides were poisoning wildlife and the environment and putting human lives at risk. The book outraged the chemical companies that sold DDT. They attacked Carson's credentials and her character. But President John F. Kennedy appointed a panel of scientists to test her conclusions, and they found that she was right. DDT was banned in 1972.

Because of Carson's work, people started to see themselves as a force that could change the planet, for better or worse. That new way of thinking launched an environmental movement of people who work to protect the Earth and all creatures that live on it.

Rachel Carson reads in the woods near her home in 1962 (above). She courageously called for people to change the way they looked at the world around them.

THE EVOLUTIONARY REVOLUTIONARY: Charles Darwin (1809–1882)

DARING DUDE

Rachel Carson sought to protect the natural world; Charles Darwin wanted to learn from it. He spent five years circling the globe aboard the sailing ship the H.M.S. *Beagle*, filling notebooks with drawings and observations of birds and tortoises, sloths and fossils, corals and clams. Darwin wondered how these creatures came to be and developed an explanation, called natural selection: A critter is born with a trait that helps it survive better than the rest, such as long legs that help it run ahead of the pack to get to the food. It grows up strong and passes on this trait to the next generation. When this happens again and again over millions of years, the process, called evolution, can change one species into another. Darwin was mocked for his theory, but modern science has proven his big idea correct.

FABULOUS FIRSTS
PIONEERS IN SCIENCE AND MEDICINE

It takes guts to be the first. These go-getting girls put their hands up and volunteered to go where no one had gone before. And they weren't just brave, they were brainy, too. They tackled new challenges—from the bones of ancient dinosaurs to the dawn of computers—and changed the face of science.

MOTHER OF COMPUTING:
Grace Murray Hopper (1906–1992)

When she was growing up, Grace Murray Hopper loved gadgets and would take alarm clocks apart for fun. She went on to get a doctorate in math—one of the first women to do so. Hopper joined the U.S. Navy during World War II and was assigned to program the Mark I, one of the first computers. Hopper believed that computers would never be widely used unless computer languages could be written in English instead of in complicated mathematical code. She and her team developed the first programming language to use English words. Legend has it that Hopper also coined the term "bug" to describe a computer glitch when her team located the source of a mysterious computer failure: a moth trapped inside the machine.

FOSSIL FINDER: Mary Anning (1799–1847)

Mary Anning was just about 12 years old when she found the remains of a strange creature buried in steep, dangerous cliffs along the English Channel. It was a fossilized ichthyosaurus, an ancient sea monster 17 feet (5.2 m) long. Anning would go on to spend the next 35 years collecting fossils, which she sold to tourists, museums, and scientists to help support her poverty-stricken family. She discovered the first plesiosaurus, another giant ancient ocean creature, and one of the first pterodactyls. Even though she worked in precarious conditions—rock falls were a common occurrence on the steep slopes where her fossils were buried—and had only the most basic tools to work with, Anning was extremely talented at unearthing delicate fossils without damaging them. She had spent ten years gently excavating the plesiosaurus. She was one of the greatest fossil-hunters in history, but today, most people—even fossil scientists—have never heard of her.

MS. M.D.: Elizabeth Blackwell (1821–1910)

Elizabeth Blackwell had decided to become a teacher, a profession deemed suitable for a woman in mid-19th-century America. But when a dying friend of Blackwell's suggested her worst suffering might have been avoided had her doctor been a woman, Blackwell was inspired to reconsider her career path. In the summer of 1846, Blackwell applied to several New England, U.S.A., medical schools. All rejected her, but she didn't give up. She applied to even more schools early the next summer. Again, all rejected her, and again, she didn't give up. Finally, her application arrived at the lesser-known Geneva Medical College in New York, U.S.A. The staff there asked the 150 male students to vote on whether Blackwell should be admitted. Thinking it was a joke that a woman wanted to join their ranks, they voted yes. When Blackwell showed up ready to learn, there was an uproar. Her fellow students threw paper darts at her, and her professors tried to keep her out of classroom dissections. But Blackwell proved her worth, and in 1849 she became the first woman to earn a medical degree from an American medical school.

PHYSICS PIONEER: Shirley Ann Jackson (1946–)

As a kid, Shirley Ann Jackson used to crawl under her front porch to study honeybees. She followed her love of science to the Massachusetts Institute of Technology (MIT) in Cambridge, Massachusetts, U.S.A., where she became the first African-American woman to attend the prestigious university. MIT wasn't quite ready for her yet: She faced discrimination by staff and students, some of whom even refused to sit next to her. But Jackson kept her focus and, when she wasn't working, volunteered in the children's ward of a local hospital to put her troubles in perspective. In 1973, Jackson became the first black woman to earn a Ph.D., in physics, from MIT. She had studied subatomic particles, the building blocks of atoms; her work led to inventions such as the touch-tone telephone, solar cells, and caller ID.

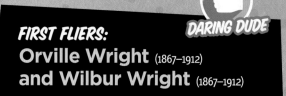

DARING DUDE

FIRST FLIERS: Orville Wright (1867–1912) and Wilbur Wright (1867–1912)

When astronaut Neil Armstrong touched down on the moon in 1969, he carried a scrap of the invention that made the trip possible: a bit of the wooden propeller from the Wright Flyer, the world's first powered heavier-than-air flying machine. It had been built by two brothers from Ohio, U.S.A., who had begun experimenting with flight controls, lightweight engines, and wing designs at their bicycle shop in 1899. Four years later, their Wright Flyer was ready to take off. Only a few spectators and reporters witnessed Orville Wright take the machine on its maiden flight at a beach at Kitty Hawk, North Carolina, U.S.A. It lasted just 12 seconds and covered 120 feet (37 m), but this achievement ushered in the era of flight and took humanity to new heights.

Jane GOODALL

CHIMP CHAMPION

In 1960, 26-year-old Jane Goodall set off for the jungles of Tanzania, Africa, to do what no one had done before: study wild chimpanzees. She had no scientific training, just a pair of binoculars and a notebook. She wanted to study the animals by sitting among them. What she discovered changed the way the world saw chimps—and humans.

Goodall imitated the chimps' behaviors, climbed trees with them, and ate their food. At first, the chimps would run away every time they saw her, but eventually, they started to treat Goodall like she was one of them, and she got a first ever look at how the creatures acted in the wild. She saw them fight, groom each other, and share food. And she made an observation that rocked the experts back home. One day, she came across a large male chimpanzee hunched over a termite nest. As Goodall watched, he carefully took a twig, bent it, stripped off the leaves, stuck it into the nest, and then pulled it out and sucked off the termites that were clinging to his homemade utensil. It was long thought that humans were the only creatures smart enough to make and use tools. Goodall proved that that wasn't true.

Goodall went on to make many more groundbreaking observations. She saw chimps—thought to be vegetarians—eating meat, hugging and kissing each other, and making war against their own species. These observations blurred the line between humans and animals, changing the way humans thought about primates—and themselves.

"WHAT YOU DO MAKES A DIFFERENCE, AND YOU HAVE TO DECIDE WHAT KIND OF DIFFERENCE YOU WANT TO MAKE."
—JANE GOODALL

FEARLESS FACTS

➡ **BORN:** April 3, 1934, London, England   ➡ **OCCUPATION:** Primatologist
➡ **BOLDEST MOMENT:** Entering the little-known world of wild chimpanzees

Dian FOSSEY

In 1963, 31-year-old Dian Fossey took her life savings out of the bank and used it to embark on a journey to Africa. She had a burning desire to see animals roaming free there, especially a creature she had only read about: the rare mountain gorilla. When she arrived in Tanzania, she met fossil hunter Louis Leakey. He wanted someone to do the same thing with gorillas that Jane Goodall was doing with apes. Fossey jumped at the chance.

She wanted to be seen as a part of primate society. She groomed herself, walked on her knuckles, and imitated gorilla calls. It worked. In 1970, one of the gorillas reached out and touched her hand.

For many years, Fossey observed gorillas from her camp 10,000 feet (3,048 m) above sea level in the mountains of Rwanda. She lived alone, her 7-by-10-foot (2-by-3-m) tent acting as her bedroom, bathroom, and office. She fought her fear of heights on steep slopes and battled disease, heavy rain, and poachers.

Gorillas were in trouble. Many local people lived in poverty, but they could make money by killing gorillas and selling their body parts to be made into souvenirs. In 1977, when poachers attacked and killed a male gorilla named Digit, Fossey was furious. She wore masks to scare poachers away, burned their traps, and confronted them. In 1985, Fossey was found dead in her cabin. Most people think a poacher killed her. Fossey's death was tragic, but her life brought the world's attention to the plight of these primates, and—though they are still in danger—mountain gorillas are a protected species today.

"WHEN YOU REALIZE THE VALUE OF ALL LIFE, YOU DWELL LESS ON WHAT IS PAST AND CONCENTRATE MORE ON THE PRESERVATION OF THE FUTURE."
—DIAN FOSSEY

FEARLESS FACTS

➔ **BORN:** January 16, 1932, San Francisco, California, U.S.A. ➔ **DIED:** December 26, 1985, Rwanda, Africa
➔ **OCCUPATION:** Primatologist ➔ **BOLDEST MOMENT:** Leaving her life behind to live among gorillas

MOMENT OF BRAVERY

This inspiring mind made an incredible scientific discovery. What happened when she was asked to use it to wage war?

THE SITUATION

Lise Meitner was an Austrian physicist living in Germany when World War II broke out. Following the lead of fellow Jewish scientists like Albert Einstein, Meitner decided to flee before Hitler's henchmen sent her to a Nazi concentration camp. Saying she was off to take a vacation, Meitner instead escaped to safety in Sweden, leaving behind her money, possessions, research papers, and career.

Meitner shook off the setback and focused on her physics. She corresponded with her chemist colleague Otto Hahn back home to continue their project: trying to create an element heavier than uranium. Meitner kept blasting uranium atoms with neutral particles called neutrons, hoping they would stick and increase the atoms' weight. But every time she tried it, something strange happened. She ended up with a lighter atom, not a heavier one. Meitner was baffled, until one day she was struck by a revolutionary thought—the neutron must be splitting the uranium atom into two smaller pieces. It's something scientists thought was impossible. But it had to be true. Meitner calculated how much energy the reaction was creating, and the answer was shocking. Splitting a single uranium atom released 20 million times more energy than exploding an equal amount of dynamite!

Back in Germany, Hahn performed experiments to prove Meitner's theory correct. He published a paper, leaving off Meitner's name to protect her from Nazi retaliation. Though Meitner didn't get credit, she watched her discovery become famous. She was thrilled to learn that other scientists were interested in her work. But then she learned why: They wanted to use the technology to build the world's most powerful bomb.

THE MOMENT OF TRUTH

Meitner was horrified by the idea that her discovery would be used for harm. In 1943, when U.S. president Franklin D. Roosevelt asked her to join the group of American scientists working on the infamous bomb-building mission—called the Manhattan Project—Meitner turned him down. She said "I will have nothing to do with a bomb" and told Roosevelt that she hoped they failed. They didn't. In 1945, when atomic bombs were dropped on Hiroshima and Nagasaki, Japan, they killed more than 100,000 people

THE LEGACY

Nuclear fission can be used for more than making bombs. The energy it creates can also be harnessed in nuclear power stations to generate incredible amounts of electricity. Its discovery was an amazing scientific achievement—one that Meitner didn't get credit for. Over time, Hahn managed to convince himself—and the rest of the world—that he alone had discovered nuclear fission. He won the Nobel Prize in 1944, and Meitner's name wasn't even mentioned in the ceremony. It wasn't until late in her life that Meitner was finally recognized for her accomplishment with awards and honorary degrees. In 1992, 25 years after her death, physicists named the newly discovered 109th element after her: meitnerium.

Outstanding
ANIMALS

Some of the bravest beings on the planet aren't humans—they're animals! You might be saying, "No way! Fluffy would rather lick a burglar than scare him off." But this chapter is brimming with brilliant beasts who stand head and tail above the pack. They've gone where no critter had gone before, lent a paw to fellow creatures in need—even saved their owners' lives. So if you thought only humans could be heroines, read on. These amazing animals might surprise you.

Anjana the chimpanzee helps look after cubs Mitra and Shiva at TIGERS (The Institute of Greatly Endangered and Rare Species) in South Carolina, U.S.A.

Laika
THE SPACE DOG

ONE GIANT LEAP FOR CANINE-KIND

LAIKA MADE HISTORY AS THE FIRST ANIMAL TO ORBIT EARTH.

Before Yuri A. Gagarin—the first man to go to outer space—blasted the Vostok spacecraft into orbit on April 12, 1961, scientists didn't know how the human body would fare in the extreme environment outside Earth's atmosphere. Would the rocket blastoff shake brains loose from skulls? Would the zero-gravity conditions shock hearts into stopping? No one could say for sure. So, before they risked human life, scientists decided to send a pioneering pup to space on a test trip.

ASTRO-DOG

Russian scientists scoured the streets of Moscow looking for the perfect canine cosmonaut. They found her in a stray Siberian husky mix they named Laika, Russian for "barker." At 13 pounds (6 kg), Laika was the right size to fit into the Sputnik 2 spacecraft's teeny cabin—just 25 inches (64 cm) across. Her calm personality sealed the deal. Person or pup, every astronaut has to keep a cool head.

Just like a human astronaut, Laika went through intensive training before blastoff. She was gradually placed in smaller and smaller crates to get her used to the confined quarters of Sputnik 2. On launch day, scientists carefully attached sensors to Laika's body to monitor her heartbeat, blood pressure, and other bodily functions. Laika's flight would allow them a first ever look at how travel to outer space affects a living creature.

FEARLESS FACTS

➔ **BORN:** ca 1954, Moscow, Soviet Union ➔ **DIED:** November 2, 1957, outer space
➔ **OCCUPATION:** Cosmonaut ➔ **BOLDEST MOMENT:** Becoming the first animal to orbit Earth

On November 2, 1957, Sputnik 2 blasted off, its canine captain inside. Laika made history as the first animal to orbit Earth.

LAIKA'S LEGACY

Laika's famous trip had a sad ending. As the world waited to hear news of the space dog's journey, the Soviet government revealed that they had not been able to build a recovery vehicle for Laika in time for launch. The courageous canine's first trip into space would also be her last. Many people criticized the Soviet Union for sending Laika up without a way to get her home. She died a few hours after launch.

Whether her journey was a worthy sacrifice or an unnecessary cruelty, Laika was a space traveler just as important as her human counterparts. By monitoring the signals coming back from Laika's body sensors, scientists learned that living things could indeed survive an extraterrestrial trip. Laika paved the way for the next generation of human astronauts.

COSMIC CRITTERS: OTHER ANIMAL ASTRONAUTS

Laika wasn't the only creature to experience liftoff. Here are some of the most famous animals in space.

➲ FLY ME TO THE MOON: February 20, 1947

The first animals to reach outer space were fruit flies launched from White Sands Missile Range, New Mexico, U.S.A., They reached an altitude of 68 miles (109 km)—6 miles (10 km) above the official border between Earth and space—before their parachute deployed and returned them safely to Earth.

➲ DOGGY DUO: August 19, 1960

After Laika, Soviet scientists vowed to never let another dog die in space. Their next canine cosmonauts, Belka and Strelka, blasted into orbit less than three years later. A live broadcast showed them spinning in zero gravity. Once the panting pair returned safely home, they were rewarded for their brave journey with all the sausages they could eat.

➲ HAMMING IT UP: January 31, 1961

After a breakfast of baby cereal, condensed milk, vitamins, and half an egg, Ham the chimpanzee boarded a NASA Mercury space capsule and took off for the ride of his life. Trained to pull levers in response to flashing lights, Ham carried out his orders to the letter—even as he sped far above the Earth at 5,000 miles an hour (8,047 km/h). After 16 minutes and 39 seconds in space, Ham splashed down safely in the Atlantic Ocean—becoming the first space chimp in history.

➲ SPINNING THROUGH SPACE: July 28, 1973

In 1972, a Lexington, Massachusetts, U.S.A., high school student named Judy Miles read a *National Geographic* magazine article describing how spiders use their own weight to determine the thickness of their webs. That made her wonder: Could spiders spin in zero gravity? NASA scientists thought it was a good question. After designing a special cage outfitted with lights and cameras, they sent two garden spiders, named Arabella and Anita, into orbit. At first, the spiders had trouble and spun messy webs. But after a few days, they adjusted and were spinning just as well as they had back home.

ANIMAL LIFESAVERS
TO THE RESCUE

The animals on these pages may not have heard of lifesaving canine television star Lassie, who never failed to rescue her owner, but these courageous creatures needed no example. When they witnessed humans in trouble, nothing—not ferocious beasts, oncoming traffic, natural disasters, or even a commercial break—could stop them.

DOGGY DISASTER DETECTOR: Babu

On the morning of March 11, 2011, Babu the shih tzu was acting strange in her home in the coastal city of Miyako, Japan. The 12-year-old dog wasn't usually keen on exercise, but that morning she insisted on going for a walk. So her 83-year-old owner, Tami Akanuma, snapped on the leash. Babu immediately took off toward a nearby hill. Each time Akanuma slowed her pace, Babu looked back, seeming to urge her owner to hurry up. When the pair arrived at the top, Akanuma turned around and was shocked by the sight. A giant tsunami wave had slammed into her town, swallowing up her house. Somehow, Babu had known the tsunami was coming and had gotten herself—and her owner—to safe ground.

SEAL SAVIOR: Gimpy

Gimpy was in bad shape when she arrived at the Marine Mammal Care Center in Fort MacArthur, California, U.S.A., on April 1, 1994. A head injury had left the elephant seal paralyzed on one side. It was only with special care from her handlers that Gimpy was eventually able to make a full recovery. A year after her arrival at the center, the seal got the chance to pay back her rescuers. Hugh Ryono was feeding the elephant seal pups one day when he slipped and fell. He looked up to see three of the pups moving toward him—fast. Unable to escape in time, Ryono was sure the seals—which can behave aggressively—would maul him. Luckily, Gimpy was close by. She rushed between Ryono and his potential assailants, giving the smaller animals a stern seal warning by showing her teeth and bobbing her head. The attackers backed off, and Ryono was safe.

RESCUE ROVER: Lily

On May 22, 2011, one of the worst tornadoes in U.S. history slammed into Joplin, Missouri. It destroyed about a third of the city, caused $2.8 billion in damage, and killed 161 people, leaving many more trapped beneath the rubble. The people of Joplin needed help. Just a month prior, canine Joplin resident Lily, a Weimaraner trained for search and rescue, had gotten sick and nearly died. Though she was still recovering, Lily answered her city's call. For 14 days, Lily tirelessly searched through the rubble to check for missing people. She faced conditions that frightened her owner, Tara Prosser, including collapsed buildings littered with twisted metal and broken glass. But Lily never faltered. "She worked without complaint," said Prosser. "She got nails in her feet. She got cuts on her legs. I only heard her yelp one time." In 2012, Lily was nominated for the American Humane Association's Hero Dog Award.

BRAVE BUNNY: Dory

One day in January 2004, Simon Steggall of Cambridgeshire, England, came home from a long day at work and sat down in his favorite chair, looking forward to relaxing in front of the TV. Instead, he slipped into a diabetic coma—a potentially deadly complication from diabetes. He could still feel and hear, but he couldn't speak or move. He was trapped in his own body. Steggall's wife just thought he was napping, but their pet, a 21-pound (10-kg) Flemish giant rabbit named Dory, knew better.

Dory, who wasn't allowed on the furniture, broke the rules and jumped on Steggall, thumping on his chest and licking his face. It was then that Steggall's wife knew something was wrong. She called the paramedics, who were able to save Steggall's life—thanks to the brave bunny. In 2004, Dory was made the first ever animal member of the Rabbit Welfare Association. Mrs. Steggall said, "I'm very impressed and so is Dory, though I had to help her fill in the application form."

PEERLESS PIG: LuLu

On August 4, 1998, Jo Ann Altsman had a heart attack while home alone. Altsman tried to summon help by yelling and breaking a bedroom window, but nobody could hear her. Her potbellied pig, LuLu, sprang into action. The super swine squeezed through the doggy door, pushed open the garden gate, and waited by the roadside until she saw an oncoming vehicle. Then, the plucky porker trotted onto the road and lay down in front of it! When a motorcyclist stopped to see what was the matter, LuLu led him back to Altsman, where he called an ambulance. Doctors later told her that if 15 more minutes had passed, she would have died. To thank her rescue pig, Altsman rewarded LuLu with her favorite food: a jelly doughnut.

Sergeant RECKLESS

HOOFED HEROINE

Sergeant Reckless was one of the most courageous soldiers in her battalion. She carried heavy loads, dodged bullets, and won two Purple Hearts for bravery on the battlefields of the Korean War. But Sergeant Reckless wasn't a human. She was a horse.

Lieutenant Eric Pedersen, commander of the Recoilless Rifle Platoon of the 5th Marines, was in desperate need of a strong and dependable soldier to haul heavy guns and ammunition over Korea's steep, rugged terrain, where even trucks couldn't travel. When Pedersen caught sight of the trained racehorse, he knew she had the potential to make a supreme soldier.

Pedersen bought Reckless and put her into intensive training. The horse learned how to ride in a trailer, carry a 115-pound (52-kg) recoilless rifle and its ammunition, and even kneel on command in case she needed to crawl into a shallow bunker to avoid enemy fire.

Reckless was an invaluable member of her unit. On one day of the fight, she made 51 trips, carrying more than 9,000 pounds (4,082 kg) of explosives in total. She walked more than 35 miles (56 km) through enemy fire, trudging through soggy rice paddies and up steep mountains. Once she learned the route, Reckless made the trips by herself. She never faltered, even when flying shrapnel wounded her.

Reckless survived the war and came to American soil as a celebrity. On April 10, 1954, she was promoted to the rank of sergeant.

FROM HER FIRST BATTLE, RECKLESS PROVED TO BE A BRAVE SOLDIER.

FEARLESS FACTS

- **BORN:** ca 1948, Korea
- **DIED:** May 13, 1968, Camp Pendleton, San Diego County, U.S.A.
- **OCCUPATION:** Army sergeant
- **BOLDEST MOMENT:** Risking her life for her fellow Marines

Cher AMI

WINGED WARRIOR

During World War I, soldiers transmitted messages via field phone. But that meant stringing phone wire across vast distances or tough terrain, which was no easy feat. So the army sought the help of communication experts: carrier pigeons.

On October 3, 1918, Major Charles Whittlesey and his 500 men were trapped in a small hollow on the side of a hill. The enemy surrounded them, and their food and ammunition were running low. If they couldn't get an SOS message to rescuers, they would all die. Major Whittlesey composed a desperate plea for help and sent it up with one pigeon—who was immediately shot down. He tried again, only for another bird to meet the same end.

The troop had one chance left: Cher Ami (French for "dear friend"). Cher Ami took off into heavy enemy fire and—like the feathered fliers who had gone before her—was shot down. The troop thought all was lost, but then they saw Cher Ami rise into the sky again. Miraculously, the pigeon was back in action.

Cher Ami flew 25 miles (40 km) in just over an hour, successfully carrying her message to division head-quarters. When she arrived, she had been shot through the chest, blinded in one eye, and her leg was terribly wounded. Cher Ami saved approximately 200 lives that day and was hailed as a hero. Army medics attended to her wounds and outfitted the bird with a wooden leg. But it wasn't until the patriot pigeon died the following year, as a result of her battle injuries, that it was discovered that Cher Ami wasn't a male, as everyone had thought. The brave bird had been a girl.

MANY CARRIER PIGEONS FLEW BRAVELY THROUGH BULLETS TO CARRY LIFE-SAVING INFORMATION. THE BOLDEST OF THEM ALL WAS CHER AMI.

FEARLESS FACTS

➲ **BORN:** Great Britain ➲ **DIED:** June 13, 1919, New Jersey, U.S.A. ➲ **OCCUPATION:** Homing pigeon
➲ **BOLDEST MOMENT:** Saving the Lost Battalion of the 77th Division in the Battle of the Argonne, October 1918

SCENT-SATIONAL SNIFFERS
SAVE THE DAY

Humans have pretty good noses, but even the sharpest smeller is no match for Rover's. Scientists think a dog's nose is between 10,000 and 100,000 times more sensitive than a human's. So police officers and rescue workers team up with canine partners to sniff out drugs, explosives, missing humans, and crime scene evidence. Here are four working dogs whose sense of smell took them to the top.

PATRIOTIC PUP: Layka

Soldiers are tough, strong, and brave—and sometimes they're four-legged. At any given time, the United States military deploys 500 combat dogs specially trained to find explosives. The soldiers are grateful to have their canine comrades' super-sensitive sniffers along. Combat dogs head into danger zones ahead of their human comrades to make sure the coast is clear. It's one of the military's most dangerous jobs, and sometimes, things go wrong. That's what happened when, while serving in Afghanistan, Staff Sergeant Julian McDonald sent Layka, a Belgian Malinois, into a building for a routine check. He didn't know that enemy forces were hiding inside. Layka was shot and severely injured, but the courageous canine kept her mind on the mission and managed to subdue the shooter. Her actions in the face of danger kept McDonald and the other soldiers safe. "I owe this dog every moment I have from here on out with my son, with my mother, with my family," McDonald said. "I owe her everything." To show his gratitude for Layka's service, McDonald adopted the pup, who had to have her front leg amputated because of her injuries. Today, Layka lives happily with the soldier and his family in their home in Columbus, Ohio, U.S.A.

RESCUE DOG: Brentagne

On September 11, 2011, terrorists hijacked two planes and crashed them into the World Trade Center in New York City. Both towers collapsed, leaving people trapped under 1.8 million tons (1.6 million t) of rubble. Human rescue workers had no way of knowing where survivors were stuck. But their canine counterparts did.

Search-and-rescue dog Brentagne was one of 300 canines that used their trained sniffers to hunt for humans in the disaster zone. Though she was only two years old, the golden retriever seemed to realize the seriousness of the situation. She tirelessly searched through twisted steel and charred ruins, working 12-hour shifts for 10 days. She also seemed to know when human rescue workers were at their breaking point. Brentagne's owner, Denise Corliss, remembers

POACHER-CATCHING DOG: Didi

Africa's elephants are in trouble. Poachers illegally hunt the animals for their ivory tusks, which are carved into figurines and other tokens that fetch top dollar on the black market. Experts predict that elephants may become extinct in some parts of Africa within 50 years.

Luckily, these jungle giants have a fellow four-legged creature fighting for their lives: dogs that are specially trained to hunt down the illegal hunters. The Big Life Foundation, which trains these poacher-sniffing pooches, rescued German shepherd mix Didi from the streets of Nairobi, Kenya, in 2011 and started teaching her to track poachers hiding in the bush. In just three years on the job, Didi brought six criminals into custody.

CANCER-SNIFFING CANINE: McBaine

DARING DUDE

Trainers lead McBaine, a black-and-white springer spaniel, to a table-size metal wheel at the Penn Vet Working Dog Center in Pennsylvania, U.S.A. The wheel is rimmed with 12 boxes, each with a blood sample inside. One of them contains something else, too: a tiny drop of cancerous tissue. Focused, McBaine walks around the wheel once, sniffing each box. Then he halts in front of box No. 11—correctly identifying the box with the cancer inside.

McBaine is a highly trained cancer-detection dog. He's been taught to sniff out cancerous cells, which give off odors far too slight for humans to smell. Even the most advanced scientific instruments can't identify them. But dogs like McBaine can. So some scientists are studying their superior sniffers to help humans find better ways to detect cancer.

when the usually obedient dog defied orders to keep working. She went to comfort a firefighter who was slumped on the ground in despair. "She went right to that firefighter and laid down next to him and put her head on his lap," said Corliss.

In September 2015, Brentagne, then white-muzzled with age, returned to New York City to celebrate her 16th birthday. She was greeted with a hero's welcome. The pup was treated to a ride in a vintage taxi, a romp through the sprinklers at Hudson River Park, and a silver bone from Tiffany & Co.

PAGING
Dr. Spot

THESE CANINE HEROES LENT A PAW TO HUMANS IN NEED

PHOEBE

JOB: PEANUT-SNIFFING POOCH

Five-year-old Sean Armstrong brings his dog to kindergarten with him every day. But it's not just for fun—both the kid and his canine companion have a job to do. Sean is there to learn how to add and read, and his Australian Labradoodle, Phoebe, is there to keep Sean safe. He has a rare allergy so severe that one whiff of peanut could make him stop breathing. Phoebe is trained to enter a room ahead of Sean and sniff out the smallest trace of peanut.

NIKKI

JOB: SEIZURE DETECTOR

Sandra Leavitt has a rare se zure disorder: Stress triggers her life-threatening attacks, but she can't always tell when one is coming on. So when she adopted Nikki, a pit bull, Leavitt wondered if the dog could be trained to aler t her when a seizure was on the way. Nikki was trained to tell the difference between the smell of Leavitt's blood when she was feeling fine and the smell of her blood after a seizure. Now Nikki can warn Leavitt of an oncoming episode up to two hours ahead of time. The brainy canine is even trained to dial 911 on a special phone in case an unexpected seizure knocks Leavitt out.

MOXIE

JOB: DIABETES DOG

Sarah Breidenbach was diagnosed with Type 1 diabetes as a child. For years, she'd begin to feel shaky and anxious when her blood sugar levels were dropping. With this warning, she could take medication to stave off a diabetic episode. But Breidenbach's attacks began to strike without notice. Within an 18-month period, paramedics rushed to her house 178 times. She needed a better alert system—and she found one in a black Labrador named Moxie. Just by smelling her owner's breath, Moxie can tell if Breidenbach's blood sugar is too high or too low. When she senses that Breidenbach is in the danger zone, Moxie jumps, whines, and paces until her owner checks her blood sugar.

ROSELLE

JOB: GUIDE DOG

Guide dogs help their blind owners safely cross the street, go to the grocery store, and aid in thousands of other tasks that sighted people take for granted. All guide dogs are heroes, but Roselle stands out of the pack. On the morning of September 11, 2001, Roselle was sitting with her owner, Michael Hingson, at his desk on the 78th floor of the World Trade Center's north tower. When American Airlines Flight 11 crashed into the building, Roselle knew just what to do. She guided Hingson safely down 1,463 steps to the exit. As they left the building, the south tower collapsed, sending debris plunging to the ground. People panicked and screamed as debris flew all around them. But the courageous canine kept her cool, leading Hingson to a subway station and underground to safety.

ROXY

JOB: SERVICE PUP

Tim McCallum was on the road to becoming a professional singer when a 1999 swimming accident left him paralyzed. But despite his handicap, McCallum is back on the stage—with his assistance dog, Roxy, at his side. Roxy is trained to pick up things McCallum drops, like a pen or his phone. She can open and close doors and press the button at traffic lights. She knows to bark for help if McCallum falls out of his wheelchair. She's not just a skilled assistant—she's McCallum's number one pal. "Roxy is my best friend," he says. "I know that I could not achieve the things I want to in life without her help and companionship."

Scarlett THE CAT

SHE RISKED IT ALL TO SAVE HER FAMILY

It was March 30, 1996, and the New York City Fire Department had just gotten a call. Firefighters threw on their gear and rushed to the scene—an abandoned garage engulfed in flames. They had just gotten the blaze under control when they saw something that would have made even the most fearless firefighter tear up: a mother cat, badly burned, slowly dragging her four-week-old kittens from the burning building.

A MOTHER'S LOVE

The cat's fur was scorched and her ears horribly burned. Her eyes were blistered shut so tightly she couldn't see. As the fire department looked on, the mother cat touched each of her five kittens with her nose, making sure she had rescued all her babies. Then, her work done, she collapsed, unconscious.

Firefighter Dave Giannelli didn't want this brave kitty's selfless act to be her last. He scooped up the furry family and rushed them to the veterinary clinic of North Shore Animal League America in Port Washington, New York. When the vets saw Scarlett's condition, they didn't think she'd survive. But they did everything they could, spending three months tenderly treating the feline family for burns and smoke inhalation. In spite of her terrible injuries, Scarlett licked and cuddled her babies all through

> AMERICA FELL IN LOVE WITH THE BRAVE CAT AND HER CUDDLY KITTENS.

FEARLESS FACTS

➔ **BORN:** ca 1995 ➔ **DIED:** October 15, 2008, Brooklyn, New York, U.S.A. ➔ **OCCUPATION:** Street cat
➔ **BOLDEST MOMENT:** Rescuing her kittens from a burning building

One of the kittens is fed at North Shore Animal League (left); Karen Wellen holds newly adopted cat Scarlett during a news conference (below).

the ordeal. Sadly, the weakest kitten died of a virus the month after the fire. The rest of the cats, including Scarlett, pulled through.

PURR-FECT PET

America fell in love with the brave cat and her cuddly kittens. Phone calls, letters, and Mother's Day cards addressed to Scarlett poured into the clinic. Seven thousand people wanted to adopt the heroic feline and her babies. The kittens all went to loving homes. The League sent Scarlett to a woman named Karen Wellen, who won their hearts with a letter explaining that she had recently been injured in an accident and lost her cat shortly after. Her experience made her want to adopt a pet with special needs. Because Scarlett's injuries meant she required lifelong care, the two were a perfect match.

Scarlett became a cat celebrity. She was honored by talk-show host Oprah Winfrey and by news outlet CNN, had articles and books written about her, and even had a special award created in her name that is presented to animals that have gone above and beyond to help others. Wellen faithfully took care of Scarlett until the cat's death 12 years later. And Scarlett—who proved that a mother's love has no limits— deserved every cuddle.

COOL CAT: Simon the Unsinkable

DARING DUDE

The British warship *Amethyst* was steaming up the Yangtze River in 1949 when it came under heavy attack from Chinese gun batteries on shore. The attack wounded many onboard—including the ship's cat, Simon—and left the craft immobile. For the next three months, it was stranded without food or supplies while the British government negotiated for its rescue. When rats hidden deep in the hull began raiding the ship's dwindling supplies, Simon was ready for them. Fully recovered from his injuries, the fearless feline pounced on at least one monster-size rat each day. Thanks to Simon's rat snatching, the ship's supplies lasted just long enough for its crew to refloat the boat and make a daring escape to sea. He was hailed as a hero in England and awarded a special medal given only to animals at war. When Simon died from a virus while under quarantine, he was buried with full military honors.

LENDING A PAW
HELPING FRIENDS IN NEED

When a pair of whales washed ashore, they seemed doomed ... until a nearby dolphin swam to the rescue. Motherless tiger cubs needed a nurse ... and a caring chimpanzee volunteered for the job. When the compassionate creatures on these pages saw a friend in need, they leapt into action, no questions asked. Some weren't even the same species!

CARETAKER: Anjana the Chimp

Twenty-three-day-old white tiger cubs Mitra and Shiva were separated from their mom when a hurricane hit The Institute of Greatly Endangered and Rare Species (TIGERS) in South Carolina, U.S.A. The orphans were placed in the caring hands of zookeeper China York and her assistant, a chimpanzee named Anjana. A rescue herself, Anjana had been by York's side since birth. Anjana began to mimic York's actions and gradually learned to help care for baby animals. When the tiger cubs came to the sanctuary, the compassionate chimp bottle-fed them, hugged them, and snuggled them to help the cubs grow up strong and healthy.

SUPER MOM: Joy the Sea Otter

Five-day-old sea otter Joy was found stranded on Twin Lakes Beach in Santa Cruz, California, U.S.A., in August 1998. Rescuers patiently taught her to forage for food and released her into the wild in December 1998. But the friendly otter developed a habit of coming up to kayakers and divers, which wasn't safe for the people or the otter. The Monterey Bay Aquarium took her in as a permanent resident. There, Joy became a substitute mother to abandoned otter babies. She helped raise 16 pups, more than any other surrogate in the aquarium's history. That earned her the nickname Super Mom—and the love of everyone who visited the aquarium.

NURSEMAID: Jasmine the Greyhound

In 2003, police opened a garden shed to discover a sad sight: an abandoned dog—neglected and starving. They took the frightened, hungry pooch to the Nuneaton and Warwickshire Wildlife Sanctuary in the United Kingdom. The staff spent weeks restoring her to health and winning her trust. Their hard work was worth it. The dog, who they named Jasmine, became the rescue workers' right-hand dog. Each time a new animal enters the shelter, Jasmine walks up to it, sniffs it, and cuddles right up. The dedicated dog plays nurse until the critter is fully recovered. She's been a substitute mom many times—to four badgers, five foxes, 15 chicks, eight guinea pigs, 15 rabbits, and a fawn named Bramble. Whether her charges have two legs or four, fur or feathers, Jasmine treats them all with equal love.

RESCUER: Moko the Dolphin

Normally it's best to stay away from wild animals, but beachgoers who splashed in the waves along the east coast of New Zealand's North Island had a friend in the summer of 2008—a bottlenose dolphin named Moko. Moko's habit of coming by every few days to play with swimmers made her a local celebrity. Then one day, two pygmy sperm whales became trapped on the beach. Rescuers tried to herd them back to sea, but the frightened whales wouldn't go. Things were looking grim until Moko appeared on the scene. As stunned onlookers watched, Moko seemed to communicate with the two whales, leading them to deeper water. Because of the daring dolphin's heroic act, the whales swam safely away.

JUMPING IN: DARING DUDE
Helpful, Helpful Hippo

In 2011, a crocodile picked on the wrong prey when it sunk its teeth into a young wildebeest crossing a river in the Masai Mara Reserve in Kenya, Africa. Just as the croc was about to drag the bleating beast underwater to its doom—splash!—a heroic hippopotamus charged to the rescue.

Although they look klutzy and cute, hippos are powerful and territorial animals that tend to attack anything—including people—without warning. (Some people in Africa believe hippos kill more humans than any other large animal.) In this case, the hippo frightened off the croc, then nudged the shaken wildebeest to shore. People on safari have also witnessed hippos saving zebras, impalas, and other animals, leading experts to wonder if these ill-tempered creatures have a sweet side.

Panda

THE MINIATURE GUIDE HORSE

DOGS AREN'T THE ONLY GUIDE ANIMALS. MINIATURE HORSES CAN DO THE JOB, TOO!

When Ann Edie, who is blind, wants to go out for a walk, she puts a special harness on her guide animal—a furry black and white horse named Panda.

The pair set off down the street together, Panda leading the way. The miniature horse carefully guides Edie around mailboxes, bags of leaves, and groups of playing children. She waits patiently for traffic to pass and carefully leads her human around the side mirrors of parked cars. When the pair comes to a traffic light, Panda stops and taps her hoof. "Find the button," Edie says, and Panda points at it with her nose so Edie can run her hand down the horse's head and press "Walk."

Having a guide horse instead of a guide dog might sound a little strange, but Panda is not the only one of her kind. The Guide Horse Foundation, an organization that matches blind people with guide horses, has been around for ten years. Miniature horses have a lot of traits that make them ideal candidates for the job. They're gentle, cautious, and easy to train. Their wide-set eyes give them an almost 180-degree view of everything around them. And while guide dogs need to be retired after about eight years on the job, Panda will probably go on working until she's 30 or more. In that same amount of time, Edie would likely go through more than five guide dogs—which can cost tens of thousands of dollars to raise and train.

Panda goes everywhere a guide dog would go, walking Edie into cafés, helping her check out at stores, and even riding in a car. She lives in the house, and when Edie doesn't need her help, Panda naps on the carpet, plays fetch, or snuggles up to her human companion.

FEARLESS FACTS

➲ **BORN:** ca 2001, U.S.A. ➲ **OCCUPATION:** Guide horse ➲ **BOLDEST MOMENT:** Acting as the eyes for her human companion

Sadie

Jim Eggers suffers from bipolar disorder—a serious illness that causes severe shifts in mood and energy. His condition used to make him erupt in violent outbursts that sometimes put Eggers and the people around him at risk. But that all changed when he got Sadie, an African gray parrot. The bird had been neglected by her former owner and had pulled out all her feathers in distress. Eggers nursed her back to health—not knowing that the bright bird would soon return the favor.

When Eggers felt an outburst coming on, he would talk to himself to try and calm down. One day, Sadie chimed in, mimicking Eggers's pep talks. Now, Eggers carries Sadie around in a bright purple backpack that holds her cage. When Sadie senses that Eggers is getting worked up, she talks him down, saying, "It's OK, Jim. Calm down, Jim. You're all right, Jim. I'm here, Jim." Somehow, the parrot seems to sense when Eggers is getting upset before he even knows it himself.

Eggers treats his condition with medications that help control his disorder, but they sometimes leave him confused and foggy. Luckily, Sadie is there to keep an eye on her human charge. She's trained to let Eggers know the phone is ringing by loudly mimicking the noise. If someone knocks at the door, she yells, "Who's there?" And if Eggers leaves the faucet running, Sadie's copycat sound reminds him.

Sadie may be an unusual service animal, but she's given Eggers a new lease on life. Since he got Sadie, Eggers has only had one incident—on a day when he left his feathered friend at home.

AFRICAN GRAY PARROTS ARE THOUGHT TO BE ONE OF THE MOST INTELLIGENT ANIMAL SPECIES.

FEARLESS FACTS

➲ **OCCUPATION:** Service animal ➲ **BOLDEST MOMENT:** Helping her human companion stay safe and healthy

MOMENT OF BRAVERY

This heroine wasn't human, but that didn't matter when she saw a kid in a slippery situation. How did she help a fellow creature in need?

THE SITUATION

August 16, 1996, was a lovely day at the Brookfield Zoo in Illinois, U.S.A. Families strolled around, watching the tigers roar and the giraffes stretch their long necks to nibble at the tree-tops. Over at the gorilla enclosure, one three-year-old boy was especially enraptured with the animals. He climbed up the railing, trying to get a closer look.

Before his parents could stop him, the boy lost his balance and plummeted 18 feet (5.5 m) into the gorilla den. The fall knocked him unconscious. The crowd looked on in horror at the sight of the boy's helpless body, surrounded by huge goril-las—who were starting to sit up and take notice of the unfamiliar creature in their territory. One of them was a seven-year-old female named Binti Jua.

THE MOMENT OF TRUTH

Binti Jua—whose name is Swahili for "Daughter of Sunshine"—was minding her own business with her baby on her back when she saw the accident happen. When the enormous animal moved toward the small boy, the terrified crowd thought they were about to see the gorilla maul the defenseless child. But instead, Binti made her way over to the boy, carefully picked him up, cradled him in her arms, and carried him 60 feet (18.3 m) to an entrance where zookeepers and paramedics could reach him. There, she gently set him down.

THE LEGACY

People were so moved by Binti's selfless act that they sent her fruit and flower baskets. She was named *Newsweek* magazine's Hero of the Week and one of *People* magazine's Most Intriguing People.

Though all wild animals are unpredictable and should be treated with caution, gorillas are intelligent, peaceful creatures that live in families and often care for each other's young. When Binti saw a child not so very different than her own in trouble, she may have reacted with a mother's compassion. What is certain is that she helped a fellow creature in need—and touched the hearts of everyone who saw it happen.

Afterword

YOUR TURN TO BE THE HEROINE!

Your tour of this hall of heroines has come to an end, but that doesn't mean your journey is complete. You may feel like you've now read about every daring deed there ever was. But the truth is, history holds far more courageous people than those that fit in these pages. And heroines aren't just historical: More are being made every day. According to a 2011 study, one in five Americans has done something super-duper, such as helping during an emergency, standing up to an injustice, or making a sacrifice for a complete stranger. Heroines are all around you. They're your friends, your neighbors … even you!

Most of the world's heroines are ordinary people who did extraordinary things in the face of extreme situations. And you could be the next to join their ranks. The only question is: When your heroic moment comes, will you be ready? If you want to put yourself on the path to greatness, you're in luck. Here to help is Matt Langdon, author of *The Hero Field Guides* and founder of the Hero Construction Company, an organization that teaches kids and adults how to unleash their inner hero. Follow his tips every day and you'll officially be a heroine-in-training.

DAILY DEEDS FOR GUTSY GALS

1) FIND MORE HEROINES

What's one thing all heroines have in common? They have heroines of their own. Luckily for you, this book holds dozens you can choose from. Use these gallant gals as your role models: Remember how they acted when the odds were stacked against them, or when they were criticized, or when they felt

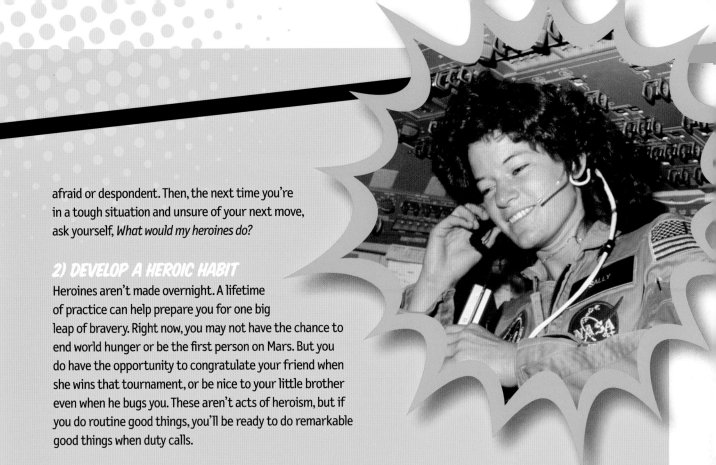

afraid or despondent. Then, the next time you're in a tough situation and unsure of your next move, ask yourself, *What would my heroines do?*

2) DEVELOP A HEROIC HABIT

Heroines aren't made overnight. A lifetime of practice can help prepare you for one big leap of bravery. Right now, you may not have the chance to end world hunger or be the first person on Mars. But you do have the opportunity to congratulate your friend when she wins that tournament, or be nice to your little brother even when he bugs you. These aren't acts of heroism, but if you do routine good things, you'll be ready to do remarkable good things when duty calls.

3) STAND OUT

People like to stay safe in the crowd. Sticking out is uncomfortable. But people don't become heroines by behaving like everyone else. They stand up and act, even when those around them stay silent—or downright disagree. The best way to overcome your instinct for inaction is to get comfortable with being uncomfortable. So speak up and tell a funny anecdote to a crowd, or wear that T-shirt you love even though it's not something your classmates would sport. People will notice you—they may even talk about you. But if you get used to doing things a little differently—and staying true to you no matter what others think—you'll be more than ready to stand out and stand up when the call comes.

4) IMAGINE

As you read the stories in this book about women who risked it all for the good of others, did you find yourself wondering, *What would I have done in her shoes?* If so, you're already well on your way to developing a heroic instinct. Imagining how you might react in a tough situation sets you up for daring deeds should the need arise. So every time you see a hero story on the news, in a book, or even on a movie screen, keep asking yourself, *What if it were me?* When the time comes, you'll know the right move.

Heroism isn't for the faint of heart. The women in this book didn't earn their place in these pages because they did the easy thing; they're true heroines because they did the right thing, in spite of great difficulty. But if you make heroism your mission by following the tips above, you too will be ready to turn a tough situation into a chance for greatness. And maybe someday, a new generation of girls will be inspired by your story to become heroines themselves.

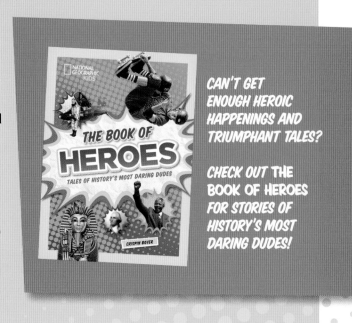

CAN'T GET ENOUGH HEROIC HAPPENINGS AND TRIUMPHANT TALES?

CHECK OUT THE BOOK OF HEROES FOR STORIES OF HISTORY'S MOST DARING DUDES!

Index

Boldface indicates illustrations.

Index

Index

PHOTO CREDITS

FOR MY HEROINES: BRITT, MEGAN, HAYLEY, KRISTEN—AND MOM, OF COURSE.
WHEN I GROW UP, I HOPE I'M JUST LIKE YOU. —S.W.D.

The publisher would like to thank the following people for making this book possible:
Becky Baines, Michaela Weglinski, Amanda Larsen, Sanjida Rashid, Rachel Kenny,
Lori Epstein, Annette Kiesow, Grace Hill, Alix Inchausti, Darrick McRae, Lewis Bassford,
and especially Jennifer Agresta, a true heroine.

Since 1888, the National Geographic Society has funded more than 12,000 research,
exploration, and preservation projects around the world. The Society receives funds from
National Geographic Partners LLC, funded in part by your purchase. A portion of the proceeds
from this book supports this vital work. To learn more, visit www.natgeo.com/info.

NATIONAL GEOGRAPHIC and Yellow Border Design are trademarks of
the National Geographic Society, used under license.

For more information, visit nationalgeographic.com,
call 1-800-647-5463, or write to the following address:
National Geographic Partners
1145 17th Street N.W.
Washington, D.C. 20036-4688 U.S.A.

Visit us online at nationalgeographic.com/books

For librarians and teachers: ngchildrensbooks.org

More for kids from National Geographic: kids.nationalgeographic.com

For information about special discounts for bulk purchases, please contact
National Geographic Books Special Sales: ngspecsales@ngs.org

For rights or permissions inquiries,
please contact National Geographic Books Subsidiary Rights: ngbookrights@ngs.org

Art directed by Amanda Larsen
Designed by Rachel Kenny and Sanjida Rashid

Hardcover ISBN: 978-1-4263-2557-1
Reinforced library binding ISBN: 978-1-4263-2558-8

Printed in Hong Kong
16/THK/1